North Wales, Snowdon *and* Offa's Dyke

WALKS

Compiled by
Brian Conduit
and Tom Hutton

JARROLD
publishing

Acknowledgements
My thanks to John Ellis Roberts and Gareth Davies, Head
Wardens of the Snowdonia National Park, for their useful
advice, and to Denbighshire and Flintshire County Councils
for providing me with invaluable leaflets and information.
Particular thanks to my old friend Hugh Thomas, member of
the Ogwen Mountain Rescue Team, for accompanying me on
the two of the toughest walks in the book. The publishers
also thank Mr Derick Cuthbert of the Conwy Valley Ramblers
for helping to update information.

Text:	Brian Conduit, Tom Hutton
Photography:	Brian Conduit
Editor:	Sonya Calton
Designers:	Brian Skinner, Doug Whitworth

Series Consultant: Brian Conduit

© Jarrold Publishing 2004

OS Ordnance This product includes mapping data licensed
Survey® from Ordnance Survey® with the permission
of the Controller of Her Majesty's Stationery Office. © Crown
Copyright 2002. All rights reserved. Licence number
100017593. Ordnance Survey, the OS symbol and Pathfinder
are registered trademarks and Explorer, Landranger and
Outdoor Leisure are trademarks of the Ordnance Survey, the
national mapping agency of Great Britain.

Jarrold Publishing   ISBN 0-7117-0993-9

First published 1998
Reprinted 2001, 2004

Printed in Belgium
by Proost NV, Turnhout. 3/04

Jarrold Publishing
Pathfinder Guides, Whitefriars, Norwich NR3 1JR
E-mail: info@totalwalking.co.uk
www.totalwalking.co.uk

Front cover: Llyn Ogwen
Previous page: Chirk Castle

Contents

The National Parks and Countryside Recreation; The National Trust; The Ramblers' Association; Walkers and the Law; Countryside Access Charter; Safety on the Hills; Glossary of Welsh Words; Useful Organisations; Ordnance Survey Maps

Contents

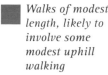

Short, easy walks

Walks of modest
length, likely to
involve some
modest uphill
walking

More challenging
walks which may
be longer and/or
over more rugged
terrain, often with
some stiff climbs

Keymap

Keymap

SCALE 1:357 143 or 1 INCH to about 5¾ MILES *1CM to 3.5KM*

0 2 4 6 8 10 KILOMETRES 15

MILES 8 10

KEYMAP HEIGHTS SHOWN IN FEET

MOSTYN to Dublin 6 hrs

Thurstaston

RHYL · PRESTATYN · HESWALL · NESTON · CONNAH'S QUAY · FLINT · HOLYWELL · MOLD/YR WYDDGRUG · BUCKLEY · WREXHAM/WRECSAM · DENBIGH · ST ASAPH/LLANELWY · RUTHIN/RHUTHUN · LLANGOLLEN · OSWESTRY · WELSHPOOL/Y TRALLWNG

Clocaenog Forest · Dyfnant Forest · BERWYN

Numbered walk markers: 1, 3, 4, 5, 6, 7, 11, 12, 13, 22, 23, 24, 25, 26

At-a-glance...

Walk	Page	Start	Nat. Grid Reference	Distance	Time
Bwlch Maen Gwynedd	80	Llandrillo	SJ 035371	9$\frac{1}{2}$ miles (15.3km)	5 hrs
Caergwrle and Hope	16	Caergwrle	SJ 304574	4 miles (6.4km)	2 hrs
Capel Curig	28	Capel Curig National Park car park	SH 720581	4$\frac{1}{2}$ miles (7.2km)	2$\frac{1}{2}$ hrs
Carnedd Dafydd	84	Ogwen	SH 649603	7 miles (11.3km)	6 hrs
Chirk and the River Ceiriog	37	Chirk	SJ 291376	6 miles (9.7km)	3 hrs
Cilcain and Moel Famau	77	Loggerheads Country Park	SJ 198626	8 miles (12.9km)	5 hrs
Cregennen Lakes and Arthog Waterfalls	32	National Trust car park	SH 657143	4 miles (6.5km)	2$\frac{1}{2}$ hrs
Denbigh and the Ystrad Valley	20	Denbigh	SJ 050660	5 miles (8km)	2$\frac{1}{2}$ hrs
Elwy Valley	46	Llanfair Talhaiarn	SH 927702	5 miles (8km)	2$\frac{1}{2}$ hrs
Great Orme	14	Great Orme Country Park	SH 765832	3$\frac{1}{2}$ miles (5.6km)	2 hrs
Greenfield Valley Heritage Park	12	Greenfield Valley Heritage Park	SJ 194774	2$\frac{1}{2}$ miles (4km)	1$\frac{1}{2}$ hrs
Hawarden Park	23	Hawarden	SJ 316657	5$\frac{1}{2}$ miles (8.9km)	2$\frac{1}{2}$ hrs
Llangollen, Castell Dinas Bran & Valle Crucis Abbey	73	Llangollen	SJ 215421	8$\frac{1}{2}$ miles (13.7km)	5 hrs
Llanrwst, Gwydyr Forest and Trefriw	58	Llanrwst	SH 798616	6 miles (9.7km)	3 hrs
Lledr Valley	52	Dolwyddelan	SH 737521	6$\frac{1}{2}$ miles (10.5km)	3 hrs
Llyn Brenig	70	Llyn Brenig visitor centre	SH 967546	10 miles (16.1km)	4$\frac{1}{2}$ hrs
Llyn Padarn	49	Llanberis, village car park	SH 577604	5$\frac{1}{2}$ miles (8.9km)	3 hrs
Llyn y Gader and Beddgelert Forest	43	Rhyd-Ddu, National Park car park	SH 571525	5 miles (8km)	2$\frac{1}{2}$ hrs
Penmaenmawr and the Druid's Circle	64	Penmaenmawr town centre	SH 718762	4$\frac{1}{2}$ miles (7.2km)	2$\frac{1}{2}$ hrs
Penycloddiau and Moel Arthur	67	Llangwyfan car park	SJ 139667	7$\frac{1}{2}$ miles (12.1km)	3$\frac{1}{2}$ hrs
Pistyll Rhaeadr	26	Tan-y-pistyll	SJ 074294	3 miles (4.8km)	1$\frac{1}{2}$ hrs
Prestatyn Hillside	40	Prestatyn Hillside Viewpoint	SJ 074818	5$\frac{1}{2}$ miles (8.75km)	3 hrs
Rhaeadr Mawddach and Pistyll Cain	61	Ganllwyd, National Trust car park	SH 727243	7 miles (11.3km)	3$\frac{1}{2}$ hrs
Rhyl and Rhuddlan	18	Rhyl, Foryd Bridge	SH 996805	5$\frac{1}{2}$ miles (8.75km)	2$\frac{1}{2}$ hrs
Snowdon via the Watkin Path	87	Pont Bethania car park	SH 627506	9 miles (14.5km)	7 hrs
Tal-y-llyn Lake	30	Tal-y-llyn	SH 714094	4 miles (6.4km)	2 hrs
Ty Mawr and the Pontcysyllte Aqueduct	34	Ty Mawr Country Park	SJ 283414	6 miles (9.7km)	3 hrs
Vale of Ffestiniog	55	Rhŷd-y-sarn parking and picnic area	SH 690422	5$\frac{1}{2}$ miles (8.9km)	3 hrs

Comments

Half way point on this walk is a pass through the long ridge of the Berwyn Mountains, 2290 feet (697m) high.

As well as Hope Mountain, there are distant views of the Dee estuary on this undemanding walk in the valley of the River Alyn.

There is much pleasant woodland and riverside walking beside the Llugwy, plus an outstanding view of Snowdon from the shores of Llynnau Mymbyr.

A demanding but satisfying walk that climbs to 3423 feet (1044m) and traverses one of the great ridges of the Carneddau to the summit of Carnedd Dafydd. The all round views from here are superb.

A walk through the parkland of Chirk Castle is followed by a dramatic descent into the lovely Ceiriog valley. Near the end you pass under an adjacent viaduct and aqueduct.

After a pleasant walk along the side of the wooded Alyn valley and a visit to the village of Cilcain, you climb to the highest point on the Clwydian Hills, a magnificent viewpoint.

From many points there are grand views across the Mawddach estuary and the walk through the wooded ravine beside the Arthog Waterfalls is outstanding.

Pleasant walking in the valley of the Afon Ystrad is followed by outstanding views of Denbigh Castle and across the Vale of Clwyd.

There are fine views over the Elwy and Aled valleys - and of the distant Snowdonia peaks - from the bracken-covered slopes of Mynydd Bodran above Llanfair Talhaiarn.

There are impressive views of Llandudno, along the coast and across the Conwy estuary to the mountains of Snowdonia on this short circuit of the Great Orme.

An absorbing walk near the Dee estuary that links a fascinating series of industrial remains with two medieval religious monuments.

Both the old and new castles at Hawarden can be seen, and towards the end comes a walk through delightful woodland bordering Hawarden Park.

A walk that really does have everything: a climb that comes right at the beginning, spectacular scenery, historic attractions and a relaxing finale along a canal towpath.

A varied and most attractive walk that combines a lovely stroll beside the River Conwy with a ramble along the edge of Gwydir Forest high above the valley.

The first half is mainly through woodland, the second half keeps close to the River Lledr, and there are grand views throughout of Snowdon, Moel Siabod and Dolwyddelan Castle.

This lengthy but easy circuit of Llyn Brenig takes you across heathland and through part of Clocaenog Forest, with views of the moorlands of Mynydd Hiraethog.

On this circuit of Llyn Padarn there are views of Snowdon, attractive woodland, relics of the Llanberis slate quarrying industry, a medieval castle and pleasant walking beside the lake.

This walk around Llyn y Gader lies between the Snowdon and Hebog ranges and there are particularly impressive views of the Nantlle ridge and Yr Aran.

A stiff climb out of Penmaenmawr to the prehistoric Druid's Circle is rewarded by superb views, both along the coast and inland over the Carneddau.

Throughout this highly attractive walk on the Clwydian Hills, mostly on well-defined tracks, the views across the Vale of Clwyd are magnificent.

The views both from the top of Pistyll Rhaeadr and of the waterfall itself are awe-inspiring.

From this most northerly section of the Clwydian range, the views extend over Prestatyn and Rhyl and along the coast to the Great Orme.

Two waterfalls are the main features of this walk through part of the extensive forest of Coed-y-Brenin.

An entirely flat walk across the marshes of the Morfa Rhuddlan that takes you from the mouth of the River Clwyd upstream to the imposing ruins of Rhuddlan Castle.

The summit of Snowdon is the mecca for all serious mountain walkers and this ascent, via the Watkin Path, is one of the most attractive and memorable

On this circuit of Tal-y-llyn Lake, you enjoy superb and constantly changing views across the water to the surrounding mountains.

The dominating feature of this walk is Telford's majestic Pontcysyllte Aqueduct which carries the Shropshire Union Canal over the Dee valley.

A beautiful walk, mainly through the extensive woodlands that clothe the sides of the Vale of Ffestiniog.

At-a-glance...

Introduction to North Wales, Snowdon and Offa's Dyke

The first title on North Wales in this Pathfinder series of walking guides mainly covered the Snowdonia National Park and also featured some walks in the Lleyn Peninsula and on the Isle of Anglesey. This second title contains some more walks in the National Park, including another ascent of Snowdon itself, but extends eastwards to embrace the less well-known but highly attractive countryside of north-east Wales that lies between Snowdonia and the English border: the Berwyn Mountains, Mynydd Hiraethog, the Clwydian Hills, the Dee valley and the Vale of Clwyd.

North-East Wales

This is a region of hills and vales, moorlands and forests, rather than mountains, although the smooth, grassy slopes of the Berwyns rise to over 2700ft (822m) as they sweep across the area to the east of Bala Lake to descend into the Vale of Llangollen. To the north of Llangollen, beyond the Horseshoe Pass, the broad and fertile Vale of Clwyd stretches to the North Wales holiday coast and the reclaimed marshlands of the Morfa Rhuddlan. To the west the vale is bordered by the moorlands of Mynydd Hiraethog, partially covered by the conifers of Clocaenog Forest. To the east is the switchback range of the Clwydian Hills, rising to 1818ft (554m) at Moel Famau and providing a succession of magnificent viewpoints over the vale. Threading its way across the ridge of the Clwydians is one of the most spectacular sections of Offa's Dyke National Trail, which provides opportunities for energetic but highly scenic and enjoyable walking before it descends to the coast at Prestatyn.

The Conwy Estuary from Great Orme

To the east of the Clwydians, rolling country leads to the Dee and the English border. In the Middle Ages, Chester, the major town on the River Dee, was the launching pad for successive English invasions of North Wales and the narrow coastal strip was the easiest way in. A whole series of castles line this route, including the first two built by Edward I – at Flint and Rhuddlan – during the

Looking up the River Lledr towards Snowdon

course of his successful conquest of Wales in the late 13th century, forerunners of the great castles that surround Snowdonia. Another outstanding castle is the border fortress at Chirk, continually modernised and occupied since it was built.

Apart from the medieval castles, other historic monuments range from prehistoric hillforts to the beautifully situated ruins of Valle Crucis Abbey, and from the cathedral at St Asaph to various industrial remains. The Industrial Revolution has left its mark on parts of north-east Wales, and no visitor can fail to be impressed by Thomas Telford's soaring aqueducts at Pontcysyllte and Chirk, and the series of industrial buildings in the Greenfield Valley on the Dee estuary, now a heritage park. At the south end of the valley is a very different monument, the well and chapel of St Winefride at Holywell, the 'Lourdes of Wales'.

Snowdonia
Here can be found some of the most spectacular scenery in Britain and presiding imperially over this array of jagged ridges and formidable-looking peaks is Yr Wyddfa, the highest mountain in Britain south of the Scottish Highlands. It is known by its more familiar name, allegedly bestowed upon it by Dark Age sailors, who when voyaging from Ireland to Wales saw snow-covered hills on the skyline and christened them the Snowy Hills or 'Snaudune', initially a collective name that later became restricted to the highest peak only.

The Snowdonia mountains can be divided into a number of clearly defined ranges, each with their own characteristics. By far the most popular and most frequently climbed are the Carneddau, the Glyders and

Waterfall near Llyn y Gader

Snowdon itself in the north of the region. The great ridges and sweeping grassy slopes of the Carneddau cover an extensive area between the Conwy valley and the Nant Ffrancon Pass and in the north descend abruptly to the coast. Between the Nant Ffrancon and Llanberis passes rise the majestic Glyders, their shattered volcanic rocks providing the spectacular pinnacles and formations that litter the summits of Glyder Fawr and Glyder Fach. Beyond the Llanberis Pass is Snowdon itself, accessible from a number of routes, and to the west of Snowdon lies the Hebog range.

The central zone of Snowdonia comprises the shapely mass of Moel Siabod between the Llugwy and Lledr valleys, the Moelwyns and Cnicht, the latter sometimes known as the 'Welsh Matterhorn'. Also in the central area are the isolated twin Arenig peaks, the outlines of which can be seen across the featureless expanses of the Migneint, looking towards Bala Lake.

On the other side of Bala Lake the Aran range comprises a long ridge running south-westwards towards the Rhinogs and Cadair Idris, which lie close to the Cardigan Bay coast. The Rhinogs stretch in a long line from Vale of Ffestiniog in the north to the Mawddach estuary in the south, and to the south of the Mawddach towers the familiar profile of Cadair Idris.

As well as mountain climbs the region has plenty of easy low-level walks. Separating the ranges are delightful valleys, like the steep-sided gorges of the Llugwy and Lledr near Betws-y-Coed and the wider Vale of Ffestiniog. Scattered throughout the area are a number of lakes of varying size. Amongst the most beautiful of these are Tal-y-llyn and the Cregennan

Lakes overlooked by Cadair Idris, Llyn y Gader below the western flanks of Snowdon, Llyn Ogwen dramatically situated between the Glyders and the Carneddau, and Llynnau Mymbyr near Capel Curig, from whose shores there is possibly the finest view of all of Snowdon.

When travelling through Snowdonia the foremost historic remains that catch the eye are the great medieval castles, among the finest in Europe. Some of these were built by the native Welsh princes, as at Dolwyddelan, reputed birthplace of Llewellyn the Great, and Dolbadarn, but most were built by Edward I. In order to consolidate his conquest of Wales, Edward encircled Snowdonia with the formidable and highly expensive castles of Conwy, Beaumaris, Caernarfon and Harlech, all embodying the latest sophistications of castle construction. These castles remain as examples of medieval military architecture at its most advanced and refined.

By far the most striking and large-scale man-made intrusions on the landscape of Snowdonia have come from 19th- and 20th-century industrial and commercial developments. Foremost among these was the slate quarrying industry which reached its peak at the end of the 19th century. It has now largely disappeared but around Llanberis and Blaenau Ffestiniog the remains of that industry have been turned into fascinating tourist attractions.

Later developments include the extensive conifer plantations of Gwydyr, Beddgelert, Coed-y-Brenin and Dyfi forests, the construction of reservoirs and the building of the nuclear power station at Trawsfynnyd. In 1951, as a recognition of its unique landscape value, Snowdonia became one of Britain's first national parks.

Walking in the area

With its magnificent and varied scenery and wealth of historic attractions, it is not surprising that North Wales is one of the most popular walking destinations in Britain. In the following selection of routes, the aim has been to include all aspects of the landscape of the region and to provide a balance of easy, moderate and more challenging walks. It must be emphasised that the ascents of Carnedd Dafydd and Snowdon – and some of the other peaks on the Berwyns and Clwydians – should not be undertaken in poor weather conditions, especially in winter, unless you are experienced and properly equipped for such conditions and able to navigate by using a compass.

So take your pick. At one end of the spectrum is an entirely flat walk beside the River Clwyd from Rhyl to Rhuddlan; at the other is a lengthy and demanding ascent of Snowdon itself. Read carefully the general descriptions of each of the walks, and the distances and approximate times, and choose those which best suit your interests, level of ability and fitness, the amount of time available, and – above all – the state of the weather, and enjoy exploring this wonderful area in the best possible way, on foot.

Introduction

Greenfield Valley Heritage Park

Start	Greenfield Valley Heritage Park, north end off A548
Distance	2½ miles (4km)
Approximate time	1½ hours
Parking	Car park at north end of Heritage Park off A548
Refreshments	Pub near St Winefride's Well, café in Heritage Park
Ordnance Survey maps	Landranger 116 (Denbigh & Colwyn Bay), Explorer 265 (Clwydian Range)

The remains of the former industries of the Greenfield Valley have been incorporated into an imaginative heritage park and provide the basis for a fascinating walk. At either end of the park are examples of the earlier history of the area: the medieval ruins of Basingwerk Abbey, and St Winefride's Well on the edge of Holywell. In addition there is pleasant woodland and attractive views across the Dee estuary to the Wirral.

During the 18th and 19th centuries, the Greenfield Valley was a hive of industrial activity, producing textiles and copper and brass goods. The industries have gone and the valley is now peaceful but many of its buildings have fortunately been preserved as the basis for the heritage park, and the former millpools serve a recreational purpose.

The medieval ruins of Basingwerk Abbey

With your back to the road, turn left to the far corner of the car park and take the path that heads uphill, passing to the left of Basingwerk Abbey. Turn left up steps **A** on to the embankment of the former Holywell Railway, built in 1869 to transport minerals extracted from local quarries. It closed in 1954 and has been converted into an attractive tree-lined footpath that runs the length of the valley.

Walk along the track, go through a kissing-gate, cross a bridge and continue along the main track all the while. The various sites that can be seen below through the trees will be visited on the return leg. At a fork, take the right-hand track, signposted 'St Winefride's Halt, Holywell Textile Mill and St Winefride's Well', which keeps parallel to and slightly below the left-hand track. Go through a metal kissing-gate and the track descends and

SCALE 1:25000 or 2½ INCHES to 1 MILE 4CM to 1KM

0	200	400	600	800 METRES	1
					KILOMETRES
					MILES
0	200	400	600 YARDS	½	

ahead is a chimney and to the left the buildings of Greenfield Mill – and in front of the chimney turn left along a path beside the ruined mill, established in 1776 to shape pots and pans from brass sheets. The path curves first to the left and then to the right and continues, via a metal kissing-gate, to a car park. Walk through the car park above Meadow Mill Pool, descend some steps and turn right across another dam at the end of the pool. Once on the other side, turn left downhill, walk through part of the buildings of Meadow Mill, which once produced rolled copper sheets, and continue along the right-hand edge of the larger Flour Mill Pool, joining a tarmac track. Pass above lower Cotton Mill and the site of the Abbey Wire Mill – the latter, now an attractive garden, used to make copper and brass wire. Where the tarmac track curves left around the end of the mill, turn right along a track, passing between the site of the Parys Copper Works on the left, built in 1787, and Abbey Farm Museum on the right.

At a T-junction turn right and pass between the Farm Museum and Visitor Centre on the right and the medieval ruins of Basingwerk Abbey on the left. The mainly 13th-century abbey was founded in 1132 and dissolved by Henry VIII in 1536. Little of the church survives, but substantial remains of the cloisters and domestic buildings can still be seen.

After passing the abbey, follow the track to the left and descend steps Ⓐ to return to the car park. ●

turns right, passing through factory buildings, to a road Ⓑ.

Turn left to St Winefride's Well and Chapel, the 'Lourdes of Wales'. According to legend, Winefride, a 7th-century maiden, had her head cut off for spurning the advances of a local noble. Where the head fell, a spring gushed out of the ground, the origin of the holy well that gives its name to the nearby town. Miraculously, the head was later reunited with the rest of Winefride and she became an abbess. In the Middle Ages the well was alleged to have healing powers and became one of the principal shrines in the country. It was enclosed by the elaborate chapel in the late 15th century by Lady Margaret Beaufort, mother of Henry VII.

Retrace your steps, continue along the road and just after passing the Royal Oak, bear right Ⓒ on to a descending path which continues beside Battery Pool on the right. At the end of the pool turn right to cross a dam –

Great Orme

Start	Great Orme Country Park, signposted from centre of Llandudno. Alternatively come on either the Cabin Lift or Tramway from Llandudno
Distance	3½ miles (5.6km)
Approximate time	2 hours
Parking	Great Orme Country Park
Refreshments	Hotel and restaurant at Great Orme Country Park
Ordnance Survey maps	Landranger 115 (Snowdon), Explorer OL17 (Snowdon)

The familiar and distinctive headland of the Great Orme rises to 679ft (207m) above the elegant resort of Llandudno and its summit, from where the walk starts, can be reached by chairlift and tramway from the town centre as well as by car. Most of it is now a country park and on this short circuit there is a succession of outstanding views that take in Llandudno and its curving bay, the Conwy estuary, mountains of Snowdonia, the Menai Strait and the island of Anglesey. Historic interest is provided by the Great Orme Mines and St Tudno's Church.

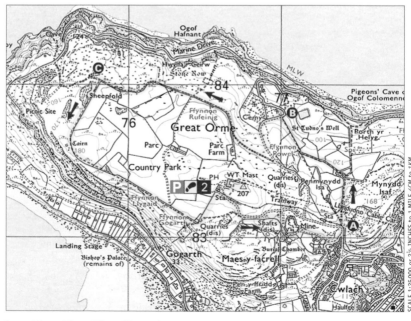

Approaching St Tudno's Church

As well as the superb views, attractions on the Great Orme range from Bronze Age copper mines and a Dark Age Christian site to the Victorian tramway, first opened in 1902, and modern chairlift and dry ski-slope.

📝 Start at the Visitor Centre and Tramway Station and first bear left and head uphill across grass, passing below the restaurant, to the triangulation pillar by the Chairlift Station, a magnificent viewpoint.

Retrace your steps to the Visitor Centre, turn left along the road and, at a footpath sign, bear slightly right to continue along a grassy path signposted 'Great Orme Mines, Ski Llandudno, Llandudno'. The path runs parallel to the road and heads downhill to reach a tarmac track in front of the Great Orme Mines, where copper has been mined since the Bronze Age. Turn right along the track which curves left, passing to the right of the mines, go through a metal gate, keep ahead and bear left on joining another tarmac track.

At a T-junction turn left uphill along a road, go through a gate and turn right **Ⓐ** – crossing the tramway line – along a track. At a fork by a public footpath sign, take the right-hand track and continue along a grassy path to the right of it to a metal gate and footpath signs. Go through, bear left, in the St Tudno's Church direction, picking up and following a track to another metal gate. Go through that one and keep ahead through two more kissing-gates – the track later narrows to a path – eventually emerging on to a road in front of St Tudno's Church **Ⓑ**.

The original wooden Celtic church on this site was founded by St Tudno in the late 6th century. It was rebuilt in stone in the 12th century, enlarged in the 15th century and, after years of neglect, restored in 1855. Turn left uphill and at a footpath sign to 'Summit' bear right across the grass. On meeting a broad, gravel track, turn right along it, keeping by a wall on the left for the rest of the route. From this undulating track there are fine sea views.

At a wall corner turn left **Ⓒ**, continue beside it and follow it as it curves left again. Now come possibly the finest views of the walk, looking across the Conwy estuary to Conwy town and castle, with the panorama of the Snowdonia mountains visible on the horizon.

Keep beside the wall where it turns left again and head uphill to return to the start. ●

Caergwrle and Hope

Start	Caergwrle
Distance	4 miles (6.4km)
Approximate time	2 hours
Parking	Caergwrle
Refreshments	Pubs at Caergwrle, pubs at Hope
Ordnance Survey maps	Landranger 117 (Chester & Wrexham), Explorer 256 (Wrexham)

Towards the end of this pleasant and easy paced walk in the Alyn valley, there are fine views of the wooded slopes of Hope Mountain and the Dee estuary. On such a modest walk there should be enough energy at the end for a climb to the ruins of Caergwrle Castle, a grand viewpoint.

In the 19th century Caergwrle was a spa town and visitors used to come here to take the waters prior to a walk up Hope Mountain. 🖋 Begin by turning left out of the car park along High Street and take the first turning on the right, passing to the right of a church. Follow a narrow lane to a road, cross over and continue along a tarmac track which descends to cross a 17th-century packhorse bridge over the River Alyn. Head uphill between houses and cottages, cross a railway line and descend to a road.

Keep ahead up the concrete track opposite, turn right up steps in front of a house and climb a stile. Turn left, continue uphill, passing to the right of the house, climb another stile, turn left and follow a path through bushes to enter a field **A**. Turn left and then turn right to keep along the left edge of the field, on the line of Wat's Dyke. Like the better-known and more extensive Offa's Dyke, this was constructed in the 8th or 9th century as a boundary between the Kingdom of Mercia and the Welsh. Climb a stile, continue across a narrow field and climb another stile on to a

road. Turn left, take the first turning on the left and follow a lane up to Hope church. In front of the medieval church turn right **B** along a track to the road, cross over and take the tarmac track opposite. Just after passing a farm, turn left, at a public footpath sign, descend to a stile, climb it and bear right to head diagonally uphill across a field. Descend to climb another stile and turn right along the right edge of two fields, climbing two stiles. After the second one, keep along the left edge of the next field, follow the field edge to the right and turn left over another stile. Walk along the right edge of a field, by a line of trees, go through a metal gate and continue along a track to a lane **C**.

Turn right along this and after ¼ mile (400m) – just after passing a large brick house on the left – turn right over a stile **D** and walk across a field to a metal gate. Go through, continue across the next field, climb a stile and keep ahead to join and keep alongside the left field edge. Go through a gate near the field corner, head diagonally across the next field and descend to go through a gate. Continue along a track, go through another gate and where the track curves left, turn right over a stile. Walk along the right edge of a field and about 100 yds (91m) before the field corner, bear left and head diagonally uphill across the field, making for a stone stile in the far corner. Climb it, turn right along a lane to a T-junction **E**, cross over and climb the stile opposite. Walk along the right-hand edge of a field, pass through a hedge gap and keep ahead to the edge of the wooded hill of Caer Estyn, the site of an Iron Age hill-fort. Turn right, climb two stiles in quick succession and keep along the left edge of a field below the wooded hill. Climb a stile, cross a track, climb another, turn left and continue along the field-edge, following the curve of Caer Estyn. Climb a stile and as you continue downhill fine views open up. Ahead is Caergwrle, nestling in the Alyn valley below Hope Mountain, and to the right is Hope church, with the industries of Deeside in the distance.

Just before you reach the bottom of the field, turn left through some bushes **A**, briefly rejoining the outward route, and retrace your steps down to the road. Turn left, follow the road to the right to cross the river and then bear right again, passing under a railway bridge, to reach a T-junction. Here you can either turn right along High Street for an easy return to the starting point, or turn left and take the path on the left that climbs steeply up to the ruins of Caergwrle Castle, which is a superb viewpoint. The meagre remains are of a late 12th-century castle originally built by Dafydd ap Gruffyd, the brother of Llewellyn ap Gruffyd who was the last independent Prince of Wales. It was later rebuilt by Edward I after his successful Welsh campaigns but abandoned shortly afterwards.

Descend from the castle and walk along High Street back to the start. ●

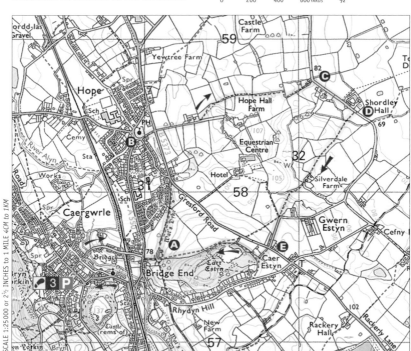

Rhyl and Rhuddlan

Start	Rhyl, Foryd Bridge at west end of promenade
Distance	5½ miles (8.75km)
Approximate time	2½ hours
Parking	Rhyl, near Foryd Bridge
Refreshments	Pubs and cafés at Rhyl, pubs and cafés at Rhuddlan
Ordnance Survey maps	Landranger 116 (Denbigh & Colwyn Bay), Explorer 264 (Vale of Clwyd)

This fresh, easy and wholly flat walk follows the west bank of the River Clwyd from its estuary at Rhyl Harbour to Rhuddlan Castle, and returns along its east bank. From the raised embankments above the river marshes there are open and extensive views across the marsh (Morfa Rhuddlan) to the surrounding hills.

Rhyl is one of the most popular holiday resorts on the North Wales coast with every conceivable type of entertainment. Of Victorian origin, it has developed a number of new amenities in recent years, including an indoor Sun Centre, and also has a fine sandy beach.

🖊 The walk begins at the Foryd Bridge over the River Clwyd. Cross the bridge and take the first turning on the left **Ⓐ**. The lane soon becomes a rough track. Immediately after passing under a railway bridge, turn left up to a stile. Climb it and continue along a grassy embankment above the marshland and grassland beside the Clwyd. All the way there are fine views across the marsh, the Morfa Rhuddlan, to the line of the Clwydian Hills. Among the landmarks in sight are the spire of the Marble Church at Bodelwyddan to the right, the tower of St Asaph Cathedral in front, and the walls of Rhuddlan Castle to the left. Cross a footbridge over the little River Gele, continue along the track which after the next stile becomes a straight, tarmac track, pass under a road

bridge and keep ahead to a road **Ⓑ**. Turn left and cross a bridge over the river into Rhuddlan. To the right is the imposing late 13th-century castle, one of a chain built by Edward I to consolidate his control of North Wales. In order to make it accessible from the sea, the King had the River Clwyd straightened and deepened and Rhuddlan became an important port. A short way beyond the castle is the only remaining part of its Norman predecessor, a mound called Twthill,

---

Rhuddlan Castle

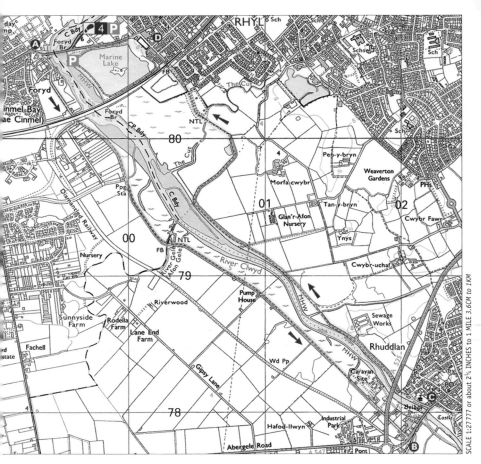

SCALE 1:27 777 or about 2¼ INCHES to 1 MILE 3.6CM to 1KM

built by William the Conqueror in 1073. The Old Parliament House in High Street is alleged to be where Edward I enacted the Statute of Rhuddlan in 1284. As a result of this, Wales was brought fully under English administration and divided up into counties on the English pattern.

Immediately after crossing the bridge, turn left **Ⓒ** along a lane which passes in front of the mainly 15th-century church. This has a double nave, a characteristic of many of the churches of the Vale of Clwyd. At a North Wales Path waymark, bear left to continue up to the top of the embankment above the river, climb a stile and descend steps to a track. Pass under the road bridge again, head back up to the embankment and continue above the Clwyd once more, climbing a series of stiles. Eventually the path bends right away from the river, by a wire fence on the left, and after going through two metal gates in quick succession, it curves left, passing to the left of a caravan site on the edge of Rhyl. Climb a stile, continue along an enclosed path and at a fence corner, turn right and climb a ladder-stile on to a lane. Walk along it, cross a road and keep ahead to cross a footbridge over the railway line. Continue along the road and take the second turning on the left **Ⓓ** – a tarmac drive leading to the shores of Marine Lake, opened in 1895 as an ornamental lake and the focal point of a pleasure park. Turn right beside the lake and follow the shore as it curves left back to Foryd Bridge. ●

Denbigh and the Ystrad Valley

Start	Denbigh
Distance	5 miles (8km)
Approximate time	2½ hours
Parking	Denbigh
Refreshments	Pubs and cafés at Denbigh
Ordnance Survey maps	Landranger 116 (Denbigh & Colwyn Bay), Explorer 264 (Vale of Clwyd)

Although a short walk, this route is full of interest and provides a succession of outstanding views across the Vale of Clwyd. From Denbigh you descend into the valley of the little River Ystrad and follow its course, across meadows and through woodland, to the ruins of a small cottage associated with Dr Johnson. Near the end comes a dramatic view of Denbigh Castle, perched on its hill above the town and vale with the long line of the Clwydian range on the horizon.

The walled town of Denbigh is dominated by the ruins of its late-13th-century castle. It was built by the powerful Henry de Lacy, Earl of Lincoln, who was entrusted by Edward I with the task of keeping the local area firmly under English control. Apart from its extent, the most impressive feature of the castle is the elaborate three-towered gateway. Most of the town walls, contemporary with the castle, survive, though the modern town has moved down the hill outside them. Within the walls are the remains of two churches. The first is the shell of an Elizabethan cathedral, 'Leicester's Church', intended by Robert Dudley, Earl of Leicester and Lord of Denbigh, to replace the cathedral at St Asaph but never completed. The second is a surviving tower from the medieval town chapel of St Hilary.

The walk begins in the town centre, facing the Library and Museum Gallery. Pass to the right of it, turn right steeply up Bull Lane, go round a right bend and continue up St Hilary's Terrace, passing Leicester's Church. Turn right, then left, passing the tower of St Hilary's Church, and then right again in front of the castle. At a T-junction, turn left below the castle walls, head down to another T-junction and turn left.

At a public footpath sign turn left **Ⓐ** along an enclosed track which later narrows to a hedge-lined path. The path descends but before reaching the bottom, turn right through a metal kissing-gate and walk along the right edge of a field. Go through another kissing-gate, bear left and head diagonally and gently downhill across a field to a stile and kissing-gate in the far corner. Turn right over the stile, walk along the left edge of two fields and through two metal kissing-gates, and continue along the right edge of the next field to a stile.

Climb it, keep ahead to a public footpath sign, turn right **B** over another stile and walk along a narrow enclosed path, climbing two more stiles. Descend to a lane, turn right uphill and after 200 yds (183m), turn left through a metal gate **C**. Walk along a pleasantly tree-lined track – the River Ystrad is below on the left – which descends, passes in front of a house and continues to a metal gate. Go through and keep along the side of this beautiful wooded valley, looking out for where you bear left off the track down to a stile. Climb it and keep by the river, climbing two more stiles to reach a lane.

Turn right uphill and at a public footpath sign, turn sharp left **D** – almost doubling back – along an enclosed path. The path descends and continues along the side of the Ystrad valley, later passing through more delightful woodland beside the river. Climb a stile and shortly you emerge into an open grassy area, passing to the left of the small, ruined Dr Johnson's Cottage, allegedly used by Johnson on a tour of North Wales. At the end of the grassy area climb a stile and at a fork, take the right hand, steeply ascending path to a stile **E** on the edge of trees. Climb it, head steadily uphill along the right edge of a field and in the field

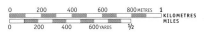

0	200	400	600	800 METRES	1	
						KILOMETRES MILES
0	200	400	600 YARDS	½		

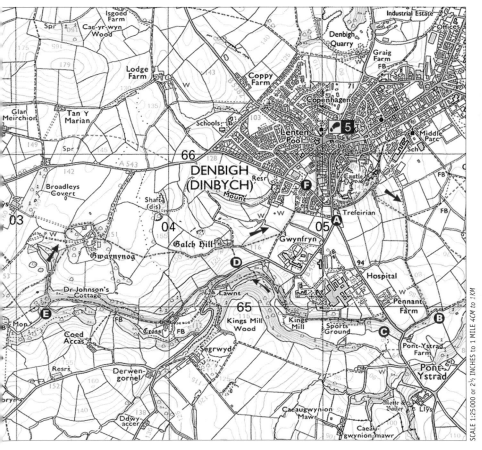

SCALE 1:25 000 or 2½ INCHES to 1 MILE 4CM to 1KM

View to Denbigh Castle and the Vale of Clwyd

corner continue along a track to climb another stile. Follow the track to the left, walk across a field-corner, climb a stile and keep ahead across the next two fields, climbing two more stiles. After the second one, turn right alongside a wire fence on the right, turn right over a stile and keep ahead along a track, crossing the drive of a large house to the right (Gwaynynog), to a gate. Go through, continue along the track, climb a stile, keep ahead across a field and after climbing the next stile comes the first in a succession of spectacular views of Denbigh Castle, backed by the long line of the Clwydian Hills. Head downhill along the left edge of a field,

climb a stile, continue down and turn left over another stile to the right of a cottage. Turn right along a track and at a public footpath sign, turn left over a stone stile, bear right and walk diagonally across a field to climb another stone stile in the corner. Bear left to continue along the right edge of a field, climb a stile and turn right along an enclosed path which bears left to emerge on to a road in a new housing area.

Turn left, turn right at a T-junction and after a few yards, turn sharp left **F** and head downhill along an enclosed tarmac path, continuing down to a road. Turn right at this point and follow the road back to Denbigh town centre, the starting point. ●

Hawarden Park

Start	Hawarden
Distance	5½ miles (8.9km)
Approximate time	2½ hours
Parking	Hawarden, Tinkersdale car park
Refreshments	Pubs at Hawarden, pub at Old Warren
Ordnance Survey maps	Landranger 117 (Chester & Wrexham), Explorer 266 (Wirral & Chester)

From many parts of this easy and attractive walk, close to the English border, there are fine views of Deeside and across Hawarden Park to the ruins of the medieval 'Old Castle' and its successor, the 'New Castle', once the home of the great Victorian statesman William Gladstone. Much of the last part of the route runs through the delightful Bilberry Wood alongside the wall of the park.

Turn right out of the car park and at a crossroads in the village centre, turn right along Glynne Way. Take the first lane on the left, Cross Tree Lane, and at a public footpath sign, turn right **A** on to a path, between a wall on the right and a wire fence on the left, that runs along the edge of school grounds. Ahead are views over Deeside.

Where the fence on the left ends, keep ahead along the right edge of a field, pass through a gap, initially continue along the left edge of the next field but later bear right across it to a waymarked stile. Climb it, turn left along the left edge of a field, climb another stile and turn right along a track to a lane. Turn left and at a public footpath sign, turn right **B** over a stile and walk along a hedge-lined track to climb another stile. Keep along the right edge of a field, climb two more stiles, turn right to climb another stile in the field corner and turn left along the left edge of the next field. To the right are

fine views of both the medieval Hawarden Castle and its later successor. In the frequent wars between English and Welsh, Hawarden occupied a key position on the border and Edward I used the castle as a springboard for his invasion of Wales. Briefly captured by the Welsh under Dafydd ap Gruffyd in 1282, it was soon recovered by the English and Dafydd was killed the following year. It fell into ruin after the Civil War between Charles I and Parliament. The 'New Castle' was built in 1752 and became the home of William Gladstone in 1852 after his marriage to Catherine Glynne. He lived there until his death in 1898.

Climb a stile, keep ahead, climb another one and turn right **C** along a lane to a T-junction **D**. Turn left along a road for nearly ½ mile (800m) and at a public footpath sign, turn right **E** over a stile and walk across a field to climb another one on the far side. Follow a path, waymarked with yellow-topped posts, through young conifers to a stile, climb it and continue through trees to another stile. Climb that, head downhill to cross a footbridge over a stream and keep in the same direction uphill across the next field, looking out for a stile and public footpath sign ahead after going over the brow.

Climb the stile, turn right along a tarmac track and after passing to the left of a farm and going through a metal gate, it becomes a rough track. Continue along this wide, hedge-lined track, climbing a stile, to a lane and turn right **F** through the hamlet of Old Warren. At a public footpath sign on the edge of trees, turn right **G** on to the track to Cherry Orchard Farm, climb a

The woodland path beside Hawarden Park

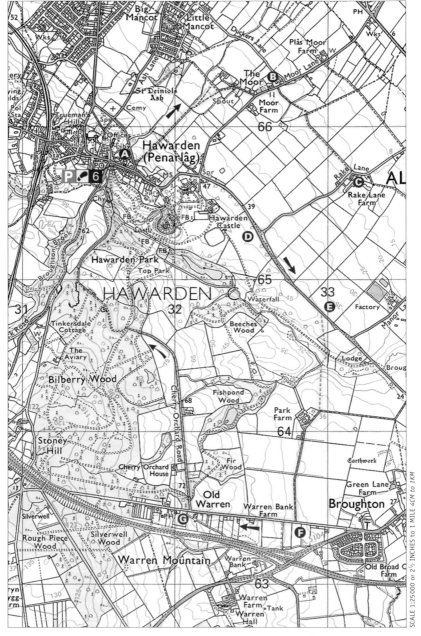

SCALE 1:25 000 or 2½ INCHES to 1 MILE 4CM to 1KM

0	200	400	600	800 METRES	1
					KILOMETRES
					MILES
0	200	400	600 YARDS	½	

stile and continue along this straight track which later curves left towards Bilberry Wood. On this part of the walk are more fine views of both castles.

Climb over a stile to enter the wood and follow a well-waymarked track running through it, later keeping along its right inside edge by the boundary wall of Hawarden Park. Keep ahead, climbing three stiles and crossing a footbridge over a stream, and finally the path climbs up to emerge into the car park. ●

Pistyll Rhaeadr

Start	Tan-y-pistyll, at end of minor road 4 miles (6.4km) north-west of Llanrhaeadr-ym-Mochnant
Distance	3 miles (4.8km)
Approximate time	1½ hours
Parking	Tan-y-pistyll
Refreshments	Farm café (seasonal) at Tan-y-pistyll
Ordnance Survey maps	Landranger 125 (Bala & Lake Vymwy), Explorer 255 (Llangollen & Berwyn)

Initially you climb up to a magnificent viewpoint at the top of Pistyll Rhaeadr, the highest waterfall in Wales, overlooking the Rhaeadr valley and the surrounding slopes of the Berwyn Mountains. After the descent, the route continues along a lane through the valley and returns to the start via tracks and fieldpaths close to the river. At the end comes a dramatic view of the great cascade, one of the 'Seven Wonders of Wales'.

View over the Rhaeadr Valley from the top of Pistyll Rhaeadr

At the entrance to the car park turn left through a gate, by a public footpath sign, follow a path up through rocks and trees and go through another gate. Keep ahead uphill, climb a ladder-stile and, at a public footpath sign to 'Top of Falls', turn left on to a steeply ascending, rocky, winding path – stepped in places – to a T-junction. Turn left along a track, heading more gently uphill, and just after reaching the top bear left, at a fingerpost, down to a ladder-stile. Climb it and head through trees to the top of the fall Ⓐ to enjoy the superb view down the length of the Rhaeadr valley.

Retrace your steps down to the car park entrance and turn left along the lane. After almost 1 mile (1.6km) – at the second farm on the right – turn sharp right through a metal gate Ⓑ and walk along a track, passing in front of the farmhouse, to another metal gate. Go through and continue along the track which curves left to cross a bridge over the River Rhaeadr and bears right to another farm. After entering the farmyard, bear right at a yellow waymark, passing to the right of the farm buildings, then cross a stream and keep along a track to go through a metal gate. Ahead are three tracks: take the right-hand one, heading uphill to a waymarked post, and then bear right – there are lots of paths and tracks here – to continue across old lead-mine workings, making for a fence on the far side. Continue alongside a wire fence on the right, looking out for a stile in that fence, turn right over it and head down, passing through a gap in a wall, to a stile. Climb it, ford the stream in front, keep by a wall, later a fence, on the right, and continue through trees to Pistyll Rhaeadr.

Head down and turn right over a footbridge at the base of the waterfall. Turn right again up to the farmhouse and turn left through a gate, at a public footpath sign, to return to the car park. ●

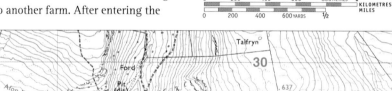

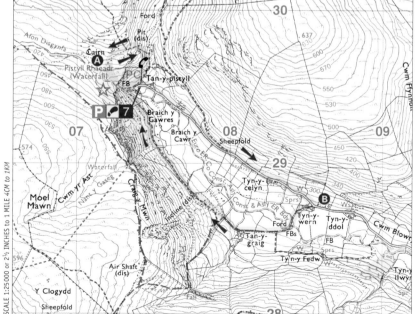

Capel Curig

Start	Capel Curig National Park car park, at west end of village near junction of A5 and A4086
Distance	4½ miles (7.2km)
Approximate time	2½ hours
Parking	Capel Curig
Refreshments	Pubs and cafés at Capel Curig
Ordnance Survey maps	Landranger 115 (Snowdon), Explorer Ol17 (Snowdon)

This relatively short and undemanding route around Capel Curig has fine views over the surrounding mountains and valleys, areas of woodland, and attractive riverside and lakeside walking. The highlight of the walk, given clear conditions, is the view of Snowdon across Llynnau Mymbyr, one of the great classic views of North Wales.

Capel Curig is strung out for over 1½ miles (2.4km) along the A5. Situated in the heart of some of the grandest mountain terrain in Snowdonia and with plenty of hotels, guest-houses, pubs and cafés, it is a Mecca for walkers, climbers and cyclists. Just to the west of the village is Plas y Brenin, the National Centre for Mountain Activities.

🖊 Begin by turning left out of the car park down to the road-junction and climb a ladder-stile to the left of the war memorial and half-hidden, 19th-century, Norman-style church. A well-constructed rocky path leads uphill across a field to a wall-gap. Go through and keep ahead across rather soggy ground – there are a few small streams to ford here – to reach a ladder-stile on the edge of woodland.

Climb it, walk through the wood and then continue through bracken, below the rocky outcrop of Clogwyn-mawr on the left and with fine views of Moel Siabod and the Llugwy valley on the

right. Climb another ladder-stile, pass through a wall-gap and follow the path up to a footbridge over a stream **A**. Do not cross it but turn sharp right beside the stream, cross a footbridge at a gap in a wire fence and head downhill to join and keep beside a fence on the left. After climbing a ladder-stile, continue gently downhill and bear left to emerge on to a track at a bend.

Keep ahead but where the track bears right, continue along an ascending path, by a wire fence on the left, to a

View of Snowdon across Llynnau Mymbyr

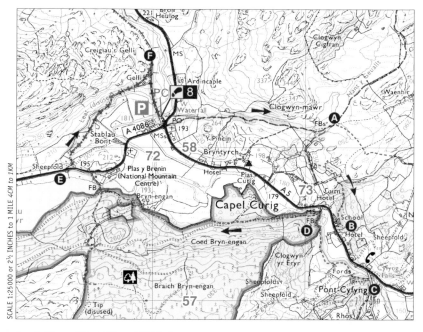

0	200	400	600	800 METRES	1
					KILOMETRES
					MILES
0	200	400	600 YARDS	½	

ladder-stile. Climb it, later cross a track and descend to climb another ladder-stile into woodland. Continue downhill through this most attractive wood and take the right-hand path at a fork, descending quite steeply, following it around right- and left-hand bends to reach a ladder-stile to the left of a school **B**.

Climb this stile, turn left along the A5, passing the Tyn y Coed Hotel, and take the first turning on the right. Cross the bridge over the River Llugwy and immediately turn right **C**, at a public footpath sign, on to a track. After going through a gate beside a cattle-grid, bear right along a path which descends and curves right to ford a tributary stream. Keep ahead across a meadow to a white walker waymark and bear left along the beautiful, tree-lined riverbank. Follow the river around a right curve, go through a wall-gap, climb a ladder-stile into woodland, pass through a gap in a line of rocks and turn right at a junction of paths below a rock face.

Just before reaching a road, follow the path as it turns sharply left **D** and heads uphill through the trees to a public footpath sign. Keep ahead and shortly after reaching the top, descend steps to continue along a track. Drop down to a junction and keep straight-ahead and then, a few paces further on, fork right onto a track that keeps along the right inside edge of woodland. Keep ahead through a gate and bend right to keep alongside the river again. Continue to the footbridge over the outflow of Llynau Mymbyr and turn right to cross it.

As you follow the path up by the wall of Plas y Brenin on the right, look to the left for the majestic view down the lakes to Snowdon, one of the finest in the country. Climb a ladder-stile on to a road, turn left and where the road bears left, turn right **E** over another ladder-stile. Walk along the track ahead which curves right to a metal gate. Go through, keep ahead to go through another one, climbing gently and passing to the left of a house, and at a tarmac track turn sharp right **F**. Go through a metal gate and follow the track down to the start. ●

Tal-y-llyn Lake

Start	Tal-y-llyn
Distance	4 miles (6.4km)
Approximate time	2 hours
Parking	Several lay-bys at west end of lake near Ty'n-y-cornel Hotel
Refreshments	Pubs at Tal-y-llyn
Ordnance Survey maps	Landranger 124 (Porthmadog & Dolgellau), Explorer OL23 (Cadair Idris & Llyn Tegid)

Tal-y-llyn Lake, hemmed in by sweeping mountainsides and sheltering below the southern slopes of Cadair Idris, is an outstandingly beautiful lake, as this circuit of it demonstrates. There are glorious and constantly changing views across it throughout the walk, but perhaps the finest are from the north side, where the path climbs up through woodland and then contours above the lake before descending to its low-lying eastern shores. The only climb – a steady and relatively short one – comes near the beginning.

Start near the Ty'n-y-cornel hotel and walk along the road, with the lake on your right, towards the Pen-y-bont hotel. Opposite the latter is the small, simple but appealing late 15th-century church of St Mary, noted for its fine timber roof. Turn right along a tarmac drive in front of the hotel and just before the drive curves right, turn left through a gate, at a public bridleway sign Ⓐ.

Head uphill along the left inside edge of sloping woodland and at a fork take the right-hand uphill track to a T-junction. Turn sharp right Ⓑ to continue more steeply uphill and at another fork, take the right-hand uphill track to reach the top edge of the woodland. Bear right through a gate beside a cattle-grid, continue more gently uphill along a broad track and where the track bends left to a farm,

keep ahead to ford a stream and climb a ladder-stile.

Keep ahead to a footpath post, bear left to a ladder-stile and, despite the multitude of waymarks, do not climb it but turn right Ⓒ along a gently descending track, by a wire fence and hedge on the left. From this section are probably the finest of many fine views across Tal-y-llyn Lake to the encircling mountains. Go through a metal gate, continue along the top edge of woodland and after emerging from the trees, bear right and head steeply downhill across a field to a gate. Go through and continue down a path and through trees to cross a footbridge over a stream by a waterfall.

Turn right through a metal gate, keep by a wire fence on the right, passing above a farm, and bear right downhill to a tarmac track. Turn left, go through

View over Tal-y-llyn Lake

a metal gate and walk along this pleasantly tree-lined track as far as a public footpath sign where you bear right on to a sunken path **D**. Bear right again to cross a footbridge over a stream, bear left and head across low-lying meadows fringing the lake – these could become soggy after rain – to a metal gate. Go through, cross a foot-bridge, bear slightly left and continue to a stile. Climb it, cross another foot-bridge, bear slightly right and walk across the next field to a stile to the right of a metal gate.

Climb the stile, bear left, keeping parallel to a hedgebank on the right field-edge, and at a public footpath sign, turn right over a ladder-stile. Walk across the next field and climb a stile on to a road **E**. Turn right and follow the road for about 1 mile (1.6km) back to the start, keeping beside the lake for most of the way.   ●

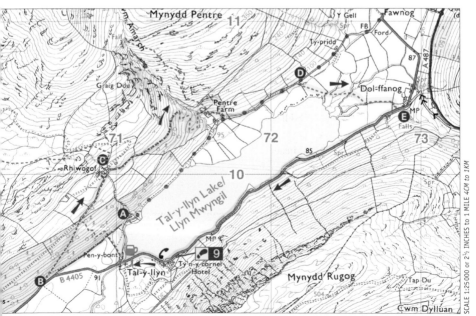

Cregennen Lakes and Arthog Waterfalls

Cregennen Lakes and Arthog Waterfalls

Start	Cregennen Lakes, National Trust car park
Distance	4 miles (6.5km). Shorter version 3 miles (4.8km)
Approximate time	2½ hours (1½ hours for shorter walk)
Parking	Cregennen Lakes
Refreshments	None
Ordnance Survey maps	Landranger 124 (Porthmadog & Dolgellau), Explorer OL23 (Cadair Idris & Llyn Tegid)

The Cregennen Lakes (Llynnau Cregennen) lie in a lonely and austere setting above the estuary of the River Mawddach and below Cadair Idris, cradled by mountains and accessible only by steep, narrow, twisting lanes. This short walk explores this hauntingly beautiful setting and at several points there are magnificent views over the Mawddach estuary. There is also the opportunity to view the Arthog Waterfalls, where the Afon Arthog plunges down a wooded ravine in a series of impressive falls. The shorter walk omits the falls.

Cregennen Lakes

🖊 From the car park turn right along the lane beside one of the lakes and immediately there is a fine view to the left looking towards the northern flanks of Cadair Idris. Follow the lane around several bends and through a metal gate, passing a standing stone, to a T-junction **A**. Turn right, pass a ruined farmhouse and just before the lane reaches a metal gate, turn right **B** through a gate and walk along a grassy path to a ladder-stile. Climb it and keep ahead, by a wall on the left, going through

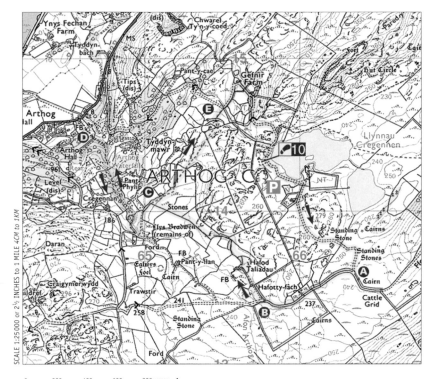

```
0      200     400     600    800 METRES   1
                                          KILOMETRES
                                          MILES
0      200     400     600 YARDS    ½
```

one metal gate and continuing to another one at a public footpath sign. Do not go through this second one but turn right and continue, still beside a wall on the left, through two more metal gates to reach a T-junction of tracks at a footpath post **C**.

For the shorter walk, turn right here and follow the directions from **C** *below.* For the eminently worthwhile detour to the Arthog Waterfalls, turn left along a walled track to a metal gate. Go through, at a fork take the right-hand path to cross a footbridge over the Afon Arthog and turn right on to a track. Almost immediately bear right and climb a ladder-stile to enter a wooded ravine. Continue along a delightful path that descends this ravine beside the river which cascades down through a series of falls. The path is winding and steep in places, goes over two stiles and

after a ladder-stile, zigzags down to join a track. Keep ahead to a fence-gap for a glorious view over the estuary to Barmouth **D**.

Retrace your steps up to the footpath post at the T-junction **C**, here rejoining the shorter walk, and keep ahead along the track, parallel to the wall on the left. Turn left through a gap in that wall along a walled track, turn right at a public footpath sign through another wall-gap and head across to a ladder-stile. Climb it, follow a fairly straight and well-waymarked path across crags, go through a wall-gap, keep ahead, later by a wall on the left, and turn left over another ladder-stile.

Continue to a footpath post, head downhill to go through a wall-gap, bear left to pass through another gap, turn right and descend, by a wall on the right, to a lane at a bend **E**. Keep ahead uphill along the lane, going round several sharp bends and through a metal gate, to return to the start. ●

Ty Mawr and the Pontcysyllte Aqueduct

Ty Mawr and the Pontcysyllte Aqueduct

Start	Ty Mawr Country Park
Distance	6 miles (9.7km). Shorter version 3 miles (4.8km)
Approximate time	3 hours (1½ hours for shorter version)
Parking	Ty Mawr Country Park
Refreshments	Café at Trevor Canal Basin
Ordnance Survey maps	Landranger 117 (Chester & Wrexham), Explorer 256 (Wrexham)

There is pleasant waterside walking to be had on this route, beside the River Dee as well as along the towpath of the Llangollen branch of the Shropshire Union Canal, but the most impressive feature of the route is the towering and dramatic Pontcysyllte Aqueduct which carries the canal over the Dee valley. The walk climbs up beside the aqueduct but the shorter version omits most of the canalside walking.

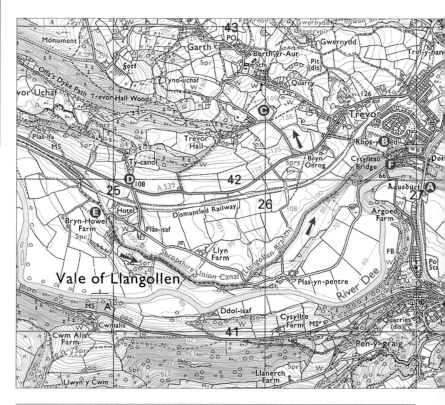

✏ From the starting point there is a fine view of the 19th-century viaduct built to carry the railway across the Dee valley, almost as impressive as the aqueduct further upstream. Climb a stile at the far end of the car park, turn right, in the direction signposted 'Country Park Walk and Aqueduct', immediately climb another stile and follow the path above the valley, with views of the aqueduct ahead.

The path curves left downhill and at a public footpath sign turn right down steps and across boardwalks to join a riverside path. Keep beside the Dee, climbing a stile and crossing a footbridge, and at the end of a meadow the path bends right to a track. Turn left, cross a footbridge over a stream and follow the track through trees – there are boardwalks in places – up to the Pontcysyllte Aqueduct **A**. Built by Thomas Telford in 1805 to carry the Shropshire Union Canal 127ft (38m)

above the Dee valley and over 1000ft (305m) in length, it ranks as one of the most daring and impressive triumphs of the Industrial Revolution.

Turn right in front of the arches, climb steps beside the aqueduct, turn left under the last arch and continue up to a road. Turn right, cross a bridge over the canal by Trevor Basin and turn left on to the towpath, here joining Offa's Dyke Path. Turn left over the first footbridge and continue along the other bank of the canal.

At an Offa's Dyke Path fingerpost **F**, *turn left for the shorter walk, picking up route directions from the next point at which* **F** *appears in the text.*

For the full walk turn right over the next footbridge **B**, bear left and head diagonally across a field to a stile. Climb it, turn left to walk below the

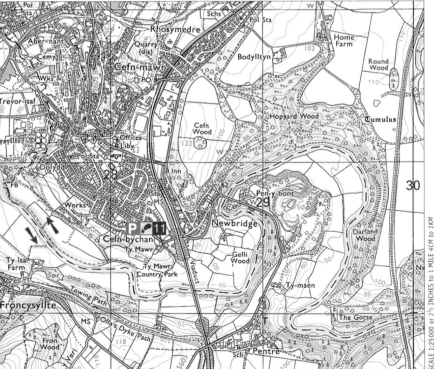

The Llangollen Canal near Pontcysyllte Aqueduct

embankment of a disused railway and the path bends right to pass through a tunnel. Turn right, follow the path to the left and continue along an enclosed tarmac path, climbing steps to a road. Turn left, take the first turning on the right and walk along a lane as far as a right-hand bend **C**. Here keep ahead along a straight, tree-lined track, passing to the right of the 18th-century Trevor church which is almost hidden amongst trees.

Just before reaching a large house – Trevor Hall – turn left, go through a metal gate and bear right to take the lower of the two tracks in front. The track descends, by a wire fence on the left, passes alongside woodland on the right and bends left to a stile. Climb it, keep ahead over another one and continue along the track to a road. Turn

right, take the first turning on the left **D**, follow a lane to a T-junction and turn right along a narrow lane to a canal bridge **E**.

Cross the bridge, turn right and then sharp right again to pass under it and continue along the attractive, tranquil, tree-lined towpath. There are pleasant views of the River Dee below and the surrounding hills, and later Pontcysyllte Aqueduct comes into sight again. At a metal bridge (No 33) you briefly rejoin the outward route but at an Offa's Dyke Path fingerpost **F**, bear right, descend an embankment and continue down steps to a road. Turn right down to a bridge for a particularly good view of the aqueduct; otherwise turn left uphill and where the road curves left just before the top, turn right along a path, here rejoining the outward route. Descend the steps beside the aqueduct and retrace your steps to the start. ●

Chirk and the River Ceiriog

Start	Chirk
Distance	6 miles (9.7km)
Approximate time	3 hours
Parking	Chirk
Refreshments	Pubs and café at Chirk, pub by Chirk Bridge
Ordnance Survey maps	Landranger 126 (Shrewsbury & Oswestry), Explorer 240 (Oswestry) and 256 (Wrexham)

After an attractive walk across the parkland surrounding Chirk Castle, with fine views of the great border fortress, the route joins Offa's Dyke Path and drops into the lovely Ceiriog valley. It then climbs and continues along the south side of the valley before descending again to the river. The final stretch keeps by the Ceiriog, crossing delightful meadows and passing under the adjacent 19th-century viaduct and 18th-century aqueduct, built to carry different modes of transport across the valley and both engineering triumphs of their respective eras.
Note that this route can only be walked between 1 April and 30 September as part of it, between ❸ and ❹, uses a National Trust permissive path which is only open between those dates.

🖉 Start at the crossroads in the village centre by the medieval church and turn along Church Street. Take the first turning on the left, by the war memorial, keep ahead over first a railway bridge and then a canal bridge, and at a public footpath sign turn right ❶ over a stile.

Follow a path through attractive woodland, looking out for a stile below on the left. Descend to climb it and head gently uphill across a field to climb a stile on to a lane ❷. Cross over, climb another stile and take the track opposite. This is the start of the permissive route through Chirk Park, only open between 1 April and 30 September and well waymarked by a series of white-topped posts. Go through a gate, walk along the left edge of a field, go

through a metal gate, turn half-right and continue across parkland to a stile. Climb it, bear left alongside a wire fence on the left, climb another stile and continue along the left edge of a field, later bearing gradually right away from it and making for a stile. On this part of the walk there are impressive views of Chirk Castle, completed in 1310 but regularly altered and modernised over the centuries. Unlike most of the other border fortresses, it has been continuously occupied since it was built, mostly by the Myddleton family. It is now a National Trust property and its elegant state rooms and formal gardens are well worth a visit. Climb the stile on to a tarmac drive, keep ahead along it and at a fork, continue along the right-hand drive which curves right to pass by a picnic area. Bear right to climb a stile by a white-topped post and continue along a track, going through two gates and climbing three stiles. Eventually you join a lane **C**, and at an Offa's Dyke Path footpath post, turn left to climb over a stile and walk along a track, heading up to climb another stile. As you continue across grass, keeping to the right of a belt of woodland, grand views open up to the left across the borderlands into the flatter country of Shropshire. On reaching a metal gate, there are more fine views ahead over the steep-sided and well-wooded Ceiriog valley.

Descend quite steeply to a stile, climb it and turn left along a downhill, enclosed track – which later becomes a tarmac track – to a T-junction. Turn left and continue downhill to emerge on to a road. Take the lane opposite, cross a bridge over the River Ceiriog, here briefly entering England, head uphill to a T-junction and turn left **D**. After $^1/_2$ mile (800m) – where the lane curves to the left – turn left **E** down a tarmac, hedge-lined drive which later becomes a rough track. From here there are fine views of Chirk Castle on its wooded ridge above the valley. Go through three gates in quick succession by a cottage and continue down to a stile.

Climb it, turn right on to a grassy path, climb another stile and look out for where you turn right up steps.

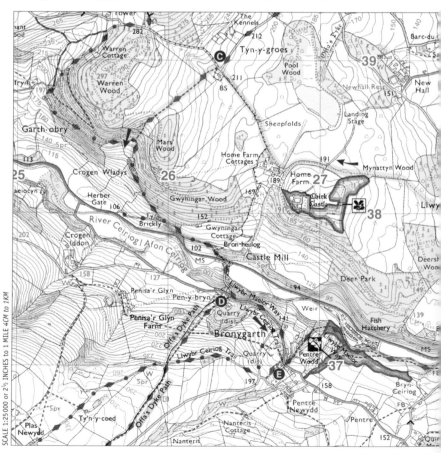

Continue above the valley, descend a flight of steps and, in front of a fence, turn right and descend more steps to cross a footbridge over a brook. Keep by the wooded banks of the Ceiriog to a stile, climb it and continue along the edge of a riverside meadow. Keep ahead

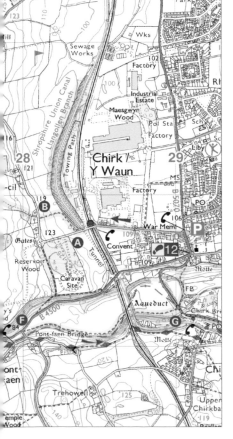

The viaduct and aqueduct at Chirk

along a track, continue across the next area of meadowland and climb a stile on to a lane.

Keep ahead to a T-junction, turn left to cross Pont-faen Bridge over the river, re-entering Wales, and at a public footpath sign, turn right **F** over a stile to continue beside the river. Suddenly there appears in front the first view of the 19th-century viaduct and 18th-century aqueduct that carry the railway and Shropshire Union Canal respectively across the Ceiriog valley. The aqueduct, built by Thomas Telford, is almost as impressive as his taller and better-known one over the Dee valley at Pontcysyllte.

At the far end of the meadow climb a stile, pass under first the viaduct and then the aqueduct, climb another stile and continue beside the river, eventually heading up an enclosed track and over a stile on to a road to the left of Chirk Bridge **G**. Cross over, bear slightly left through a metal gate, at a public footpath sign, and walk along a track. Where it curves to the right, keep ahead along an enclosed path, climb a stile, turn right over a ditch and then turn left alongside it. Bear right to head uphill along a grassy path, climb a stile, and turn right along a road to return to the start. ●

Prestatyn Hillside

Start	Prestatyn Hillside Viewpoint car park, ½ mile (800m) north of Gwaenysgor
Distance	5½ miles (8.75km)
Approximate time	3 hours
Parking	Prestatyn Hillside Viewpoint
Refreshments	Pub at Gwaenysgor
Ordnance Survey maps	Landranger 116 (Denbigh & Colwyn Bay), Explorers 264 (Vale of Clwyd) and 265 (Clwydian Range)

On this walk in the most northerly part of the Clwydian Hills, there are extensive views over Prestatyn (which lies immediately below), Rhyl, the Vale of Clwyd and the North Wales coast. Most of the second half of the route uses first a disused railway track, and later the last stretch of Offa's Dyke Path as it climbs above Bishopswood which clothes the steep hillside.

From the car park there are fine and extensive views over Prestatyn and Rhyl and along the coast towards the Great Orme. 🖉 Start by turning right out of the car park and walking along the lane into the quiet village of Gwaenysgor. Just past the village green turn right Ⓐ along a lane, passing to the left of the small church, and a few yards after the lane becomes a rough track, turn left over a stone stile and walk along a path, between a wall – later a hedge – on the left and a wire fence on the right.

Climb a stone stile, bear right to keep along the right edge of a field, climb a stile, bear left and head diagonally across a field to climb a stone stile on to a lane Ⓑ. Turn right along the lane for ¾ mile (1.2km). As this lane descends, fine views open up of the prominent hill of Graig Fawr to the right and over the Vale of Clwyd ahead. Just before reaching a National Trust car park, turn left along another lane Ⓒ and after

¼ mile (400m), turn right over a stile. Walk across a field, climb a stile and keep along the top edge of a sloping field, heading gently downhill. At the bottom follow the track to the left and after 100 yds (91m), turn right down steps and over a stile. Descend through a belt of trees, keep ahead across a field and climb a stile on the far side. Bear left, cross a bridge over a disused railway, walk across a field, climb a metal stile and descend some steps to a lane. Turn right, cross a bridge over the disused railway again, turn right through a gate Ⓓ and descend to the former track. The railway originally ran between Prestatyn and Dyserth, and it has now been converted into an attractive walkway.

Turn right on to the tree-lined track and follow it for 1¼ miles (2km), passing through several barriers and below beautiful steep-sided woodland on the right. On reaching a crossroads of paths, turn right through a kissing-

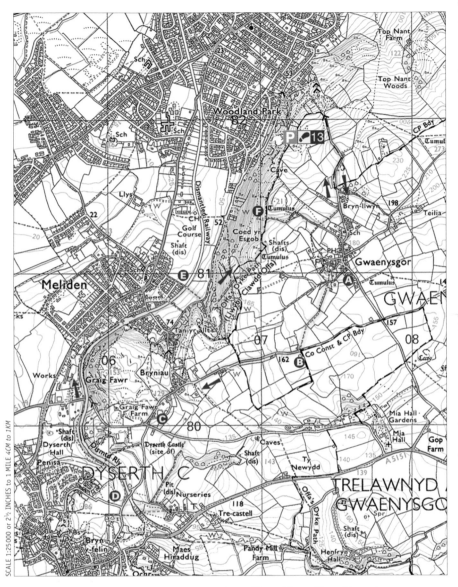

gate **E** and head gently uphill across a field. At the top climb a stile, keep ahead steeply uphill along a narrow lane, and where this lane peters out below a quarry, continue along a steep woodland track beside the quarry. Go through a kissing-gate, keep ahead to a T-junction and turn left to join Offa's Dyke Path.

Follow the well-waymarked path through trees and gorse, climbing all the while – steeply at times – above the beautiful woodland of Bishopswood (Coed yr Esgob), once owned by the bishops of St Asaph. Go through a hedge gap at a finger-post, and as you continue steeply uphill between more trees and gorse along a path, stepped in places, superb views open up along the coast, with the mountains of Snowdonia and the island of Anglesey visible on the horizon. The path descends slightly, climbs again and at the next footpath sign, turn right over a stile **F** and walk along the right edge of a field. Gwaenysgor is seen over to the right.

Head gently downhill, continue between gorse and trees to a stile, climb it and continue along an enclosed path.

At a crossroads of paths opposite a stone stile on the right, turn left up steps to climb a stile and walk across a field to climb another one. Keep along the right edge of the next field, climb a stile on to a lane and turn left to return to the start. ●

The disused railway track through Bishopswood

Llyn y Gader and Beddgelert Forest

Start	Rhyd-Ddu, National Park car park
Distance	5 miles (8km)
Approximate time	2½ hours
Parking	Rhyd-Ddu
Refreshments	Pub at Rhyd-Ddu, ¼ mile (400m) north of starting point
Ordnance Survey maps	Landranger 115 (Snowdon), Explorer OL17 (Snowdon)

This walk is through terrain that lies just to the west of Snowdon, and the last part of it uses a section of the Rhyd-Ddu Path, which is one of the most popular routes to the summit of Wales' highest mountain. For much of the way the austere Llyn y Gader is in sight, and there are dramatic views of Mynydd Mawr, the Nantlle ridge and Moel Hebog to the west, and Yr Aran, the most southerly peak of the Snowdon range, to the east. The route also touches the northern fringes of the extensive Beddgelert Forest.

From the car park cross the road and go through a metal kissing-gate at a public footpath sign. As you walk along a slabbed path there is an imposing view ahead of the precipitous cliffs of Y Garn, part of the Nantlle ridge. On reaching the Afon Gwyrfai, follow the path to the left and then turn right to cross a footbridge over the river.

Climb a ladder-stile and turn right along a path which crosses a track to the left of a whitewashed farmhouse and continues across rough grass to join another track. Walk along the track, climb a ladder-stile on to a road and immediately turn left **A** through a metal gate, at a public bridleway sign, and continue along a path by a low wall and wire fence on the right. Head up to climb a ladder-stile and continue to a large boulder with white arrows painted on it. On the next part of the route you enjoy fine views of the Nantlle ridge ahead, and to the left across Llyn y Gader to Yr Aran.

Continue past the boulder – the route here is marked by a series of white arrows on rocks – heading steadily uphill all the while, ford two streams and pass a spectacular waterfall to eventually reach a ladder-stile. Climb it, keep ahead to enter the conifers of Beddgelert Forest, pass through a wall-gap and descend to a crossroads **B**. Turn left and continue steadily downhill along a wide and curving track, initially along the left inside edge of the forest and later through the trees. At a T-junction, turn left and continue steadily downhill, passing beside a barrier and keeping ahead to a road **C**. Turn left and after nearly ½ mile (800m), turn right **D** through a metal gate at a public footpath sign to Snowdon. Walk along a tarmac drive which bends left up to Ffridd Uchaf farm, go through a metal gate, turn right between farm buildings and bear

The imposing profile of Y Garn

```
0     200    400    600   800 METRES  1
                                        KILOMETRES
                                        MILES
0     200    400    600 YARDS    ½
```

left to a gate. Go through, head uphill, by a wall bordering a conifer wood on the left, go through a metal kissing-gate and continue uphill. To the right are grand views of Snowdon, and to the left Llyn y Gader, Y Garn and the Nantlle ridge come into view again.

Climb a ladder-stile, keep ahead across grassy moorland – although the path is only faint there are regular marker-stones – and pass to the right of a group of rocks to reach a T-junction in front of a wall **E**. Turn left to join the Rhyd-Ddu Path and descend between rocks to a ladder-stile. Climb it and as you continue steadily downhill along a winding path, glorious views open up looking along the length of Llyn Cwellyn towards Caernarfon and the Menai Strait.

Climb two more ladder-stiles, keep ahead between old quarry workings, pass beside a metal barrier and continue to a metal kissing-gate. Go through and turn left along a track back to the start.●

Elwy Valley

Start	Llanfair Talhaiarn
Distance	5 miles (8km)
Approximate time	2½ hours
Parking	Llanfair Talhaiarn
Refreshments	Pubs at Llanfair Talhaiarn
Ordnance Survey maps	Landranger 116 (Denbigh & Colwyn Bay), Explorer 264 (Vale of Clwyd)

The walk is basically a circuit of Mynydd Bodran, the prominent hill that rises to nearly 950ft (289m) above the Elwy and Aled valleys, and provides some superb views. After a pleasant opening stretch by the River Elwy, the route contours along the side of the hill before heading over it and finally descending back into Llanfair Talhaiarn. Route-finding should present no difficulties despite the virtual absence of footpath signs, but the walk should not be attempted in misty weather as the highest part of it is across pathless, bracken-covered moorland where it is essential to be able to see certain landmarks.

The walk begins by the old bridge over the River Elwy on the edge of the pleasant village of Llanfair Talhaiarn. Turn left over the bridge and immediately turn right, at a public footpath sign, on to a riverside path. Ascend steps to climb a stile, cross a road, descend steps to climb another stile and continue along the right edge of meadows beside the river, climbing a stile and following the curve of the river to the left. Climb another stile and turn right to cross a footbridge over the Elwy. Turn left, climb a stile and ascend a steep and potentially slippery path through trees – a wire fence and hand-rail on the left is helpful – bending right to emerge on to a lane Ⓐ. Turn left along the lane, which curves right, and where it ends by a cottage keep ahead uphill along an enclosed path to a metal gate.

Go through and continue along an undulating path – narrow and engulfed by bracken at times, but discernible – that contours along the side of Mynydd Bodran, passing through a series of gates. The views from here over the hilly and well-wooded Elwy and Aled valleys are most attractive. On meeting a track bear right along it, going through three metal gates, and after the third one you reach a T-junction Ⓑ. Turn right, at a fork take the right-hand upper track and go through an electric metal gate; clear operating instructions are provided. Pass between a house and outbuildings, go through a metal gate, bear right and head uphill across a field, later bearing left and making for a metal gate in the top corner. Go through and continue straight ahead to another metal gate. Go through, continue diagonally uphill across the next field,

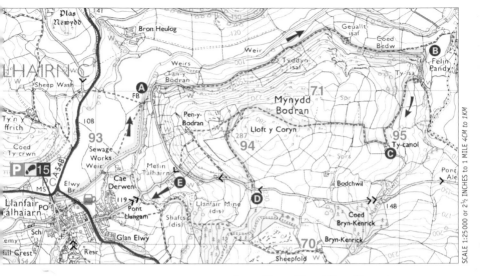

climb a stile and turn left through a metal gate towards Ty-canol Farm. Almost immediately turn right **C** through a metal gate, head uphill along the right edge of a field, turn right through another metal gate in the field corner and walk along the right edge of the next field. Follow the field edge to the left, go through a metal gate, continue uphill by a wire fence along the right edge of the next field and climb a waymarked stile just to the left

0   200   400   600   800 METRES   1
                             KILOMETRES
                             MILES
0   200   400   600 YARDS   ½

SCALE 1:25000 or 2½ INCHES to 1 MILE 4CM to 1KM

of the corner. Now comes a difficult part of the walk as you continue across the pathless, bracken-covered slopes on the top of Mynydd Bodran. In summer the bracken can be waist-high but there are 'islands' of smooth grass dotted with gorse to ease the way. Do not head up to the highest points but bear right, keeping along the edge of the bracken, descending towards a wire fence and looking out for a waymarked stile to the right of a fence corner. Ahead are grand

Looking over the Elwy Valley

views of Llanfair Talhaiarn below in the valley and the outline of the Snowdonia mountains on the horizon. After locating the stile, climb it and walk along the right edge of a field, by a hedge-bank on the right. Follow the field edge to the left, continue up to go through a metal gate and keep ahead along a track, passing to the left of a cottage. The track leads down, via another metal gate, to a lane **D**. Turn right, follow the winding lane steeply downhill and turn left **E** to continue down towards Llanfair Talhaiarn. At a crossroads turn right and just before reaching Elwy Bridge, turn left through a metal kissing-gate, at a public footpath sign.

Walk along an enclosed, tree-lined, tarmac path which continues between buildings and bears left to emerge into the village square. Turn right to return to the start. ●

Llanfair Talhaiarn

Llyn Padarn

Start	Llanberis, village car park beside Llyn Padarn
Distance	5½ miles (8.9km)
Approximate time	3 hours
Parking	Village car park at Llanberis
Refreshments	Pubs and cafés at Llanberis
Ordnance Survey maps	Landranger 115 (Snowdon),Explorers OL17 (Snowdon) and 263 (Anglesey East)

Llyn Padarn is situated at the foot of Snowdon and this straightforward circuit of the lake, which utilises a combination of a disused railway track, lane, woodland and lakeside paths and old quarry tracks, provides a series of memorable views of the surrounding mountains, including spectacular ones of Snowdon itself, for relatively little effort. As well as pleasant walking beside the lake, there is attractive woodland on the slopes above its eastern side, interesting remains of the slate-quarrying industry that once dominated this part of Snowdonia, and a brief detour to the ruins of Dolbadarn Castle which occupy a commanding position between Llyn Padarn and the adjacent Llyn Peris.

Its splendid situation below Snowdon and between two lakes has enabled the former slate-quarrying village of Llanberis to become a major tourist resort and walking centre. It is the starting point for ascents of Snowdon, both on foot and by the Snowdon Mountain Railway. There is another railway that runs along the shore of Llyn Padarn, and the many physical remains of the once great slate-quarrying industry only add to its appeal and interest.

Start by walking down to the lake and turn left on to a path which curves left to the road. Turn right and take the first turning on the right **A** to continue along a broad tarmac drive, the bed of a former railway. After passing through a barrier, the drive becomes a rough, tree-lined track (Lon Las Peris) which keeps beside Llyn Padarn. Pass under a road bridge and on emerging on to the road, turn sharp right and shortly turn sharp left over a ladder-stile. Walk along a tarmac path, by a wall on the right – later a parallel lane appears on the left – climb two more ladder-stiles and at a road junction, turn right to cross an attractive old bridge at the foot of the lake. From here there is a magnificent view looking down the length of the lake towards the Llanberis Pass, with the summit of Snowdon clearly visible.

Turn right **B** along a narrow lane, signposted to Fachwen, which climbs steadily through woodland above the lake and after 1 mile (1.6km) – just after passing a telephone box – turn right **C**

SCALE 1:25000 or 2½ INCHES to 1 MILE 4CM to 1KM

```
0      200    400    600   800 METRES  1
                                        KILOMETRES
                                        MILES
0      200    400   600 YARDS   ½
```

at a public footpath sign, through a
metal gate on to a path that descends
through trees. Shortly it becomes a
track which curves downhill through
beautiful woodland and passes under an
old quarry bridge to reach a footbridge
over a tumbling stream.

Cross it, turn right, then turn left
through a kissing-gate and head
steadily uphill, via steps in places, to a
superb viewpoint overlooking the lake.
Now the path descends again, at a fork
take the right-hand, lower, slabbed
path, pass through a wall-gap and

continue across a terrace in front of the
Quarry Hospital, now a visitor centre
but once the hospital for the employees
of the Dinorwic Quarry Company. Head
downhill along a tarmac track, go under
an arch and pass below the former
workings of Vivian Quarry with a pool
below. The quarry was named after
W.W. Vivian, who was manager of the
Dinorwic Quarry Company at the end of
the 19th century.

Just where the track curves right to
pass under a bridge, turn right on to a
walled path, cross the quarry railway line
and continue down steps and under an
arch to reach a road in front of the Welsh
Slate Museum. This is housed in the

former workshops of the Dinorwic Quarry Company and contains much of the original machinery, including a large water-wheel. At their height in the Victorian era, when demand for Welsh slate was at its greatest, the Dinorwic quarries were the largest anywhere in the world and employed over 3000 men. The Llanberis Lake Railway, the terminus of which is next to the museum, was constructed to carry the slate to the docks at Port Dinorwic on the Menai Strait. The quarries closed down in 1969.

Turn left along the road, keep along it to a T-junction, passing through a tall, arched, metal gate, and turn right **D** to cross a bridge over the foot of Llyn Peris. Turn left down steps, cross a footbridge over a stream, go through a metal gate and follow a path up steps to

Dolbadarn Castle, whose circular keep, situated on a rocky knoll above the lake, still guards the southern end of the Llanberis Pass. It is a native Welsh castle, built by Llewellyn the Great in the early 13th century.

Retrace your steps to the road, cross over, go down some steps opposite into a car park and on the far side of the car park go through a metal kissing-gate, by a sign to Padarn Park. The path curves right across grass towards a bridge. At a T-junction of paths turn right and just before the bridge, turn left on to a grassy path **E**. Follow this path across delightful meadows bordering Llyn Padarn towards Llanberis, passing through several metal kissing-gates and over footbridges. Finally walk through a car park and picnic area and continue beside the lake to return to the start. ●

Looking towards Snowdon from Llyn Padarn

Lledr Valley

Start	Dolwyddelan
Distance	6½ miles (10.5km)
Approximate time	3 hours
Parking	Dolwyddelan, car park and picnic area by station
Refreshments	Pubs and cafés at Dolwyddelan
Ordnance Survey maps	Landranger 115 (Snowdon), Explorer OL18 (Harlech, Porthmadog & Bala)

This is a walk that provides a succession of outstanding views over the surrounding mountains, especially of Moel Siabod and Snowdon, plus attractive woodland and riverside walking, for only a modest effort. The first half is along a broad and undulating track, much of it through woodland, and the return is along tree-lined paths and lanes and across lush meadows bordering the lovely River Lledr.

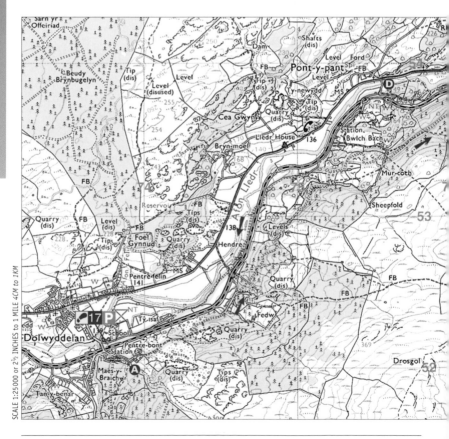

SCALE 1:25000 or 2½ INCHES to 1 MILE 4CM to 1KM

The village of Dolwyddelan is situated below the spectacular rugged slopes of Moel Siabod in the Lledr valley. It has a small, largely unrestored 16th-century church, and about ¾ mile (1.2km) to the east is Dolwyddelan Castle, reputed birthplace of Llewellyn the Great. The castle is in sight for much of this route and was one of the principal residences of the princes of Gwynedd. During the English conquest it was occupied by Llewellyn ap Gruffydd, last native prince of Wales, before being captured by Edward I in 1282. At the end of the Middle Ages it fell into disuse and ruin; the main surviving parts are the fine 12th-century keep, which was partially rebuilt in the 19th century, and the 13th-century west tower.

🏛 Start by turning left out of the car park and picnic area, turn left again to cross the railway bridge and at a T-junction bear left along a lane. Walk uphill and where the lane ends by the last house, turn left on to a track, **A** passing in front of houses.

Keep along this clear, broad, winding and gently undulating track for the next 2½ miles (4km), negotiating several gates and stiles. At the start there are some abandoned slate-quarries and for much of the way the track passes through attractive woodland. The more open stretches provide some superb views to the left across the Lledr valley, with Snowdon and Moel Siabod prominent on the skyline, plus the impressively sited Dolwyddelan Castle. Because of the lack of waymarks, it is necessary to look out carefully for where a slatey path crosses the track diagonally. Turn sharp left **B** on to it, almost doubling back, and the path heads down through trees and bears right to pass under a railway bridge to a gate. Go through, walk along an enclosed track which descends towards a farm, bear right in front of the farmhouse and after going through two gates, the path turns left **C** alongside the foaming, rushing waters of the River Lledr.

Keep beside the tree-shaded riverbank to a ladder-stile, climb it, continue uphill through dense woodland and later bear right and gently descend along a walled path to a gate. Go through, head down to go through another one and continue once more beside the Lledr. The riverside path – boggy in places – leads to a T-junction where you turn right through a metal gate, cross a drive and continue along an enclosed uphill path to emerge on to a tarmac drive. Continue uphill along it, passing to the left of an hotel, to join a narrow lane **D** and keep along the lane, passing Pont-y-pant station, to where it ends at a farm. Keep ahead through a metal gate and walk along an undulating track, later keeping beside the railway line on the right. Go through a metal gate, turn right through another to pass under a railway bridge and turn left along a path across lovely riverside meadows. Now come more splendid views of the river, Moel Siabod and Snowdon.

Pass to the right of farm buildings, go through a gate and keep ahead along a track, passing by an attractive old clapper-bridge over the Lledr on the right. The tarmac track continues across meadows, keeps to the left of another farm – there are some gates to negotiate here – and leads directly back to the starting point. ●

The Lledr Valley

Vale of Ffestiniog

Start	Rhŷd-y-sarn parking and picnic area, beside A496, ½ mile (800m) north of its junction with B4391
Distance	5½ miles (8.9km)
Approximate time	3 hours
Parking	Rhŷd-y-sarn
Refreshments	Pubs at Maentwrog
Ordnance Survey maps	Landranger 124 (Dolgellau & Porthmadog), Explorer OL18 (Harlech, Porthmadog & Bala)

The first part of the walk is through the delightful, dense, steep-sided woodlands that clothe the northern slopes of the Vale of Ffestiniog, part of the Coedydd Maentwrog National Nature Reserve. There is a succession of superb views down the vale and on several occasions the path crosses the track of the steam-hauled Ffestiniog Railway. After descending into the valley and making a brief detour into Maentwrog, the route continues by the Afon Dwyryd before a final wooded stretch. Although this is not a lengthy or strenuous walk, there is quite a lot of climbing, especially on the first stage.

Facing the picnic site – on the opposite side of the road from the parking area – turn right, almost immediately turn left along a track, at a public footpath sign, and go through a metal gate. The track curves to the left – where it ends, keep ahead along a path to go through a metal gate. Bear left to the Afon Goedol and turn right to go through another metal gate, entering the Coedydd Maentwrog National Nature Reserve. This is an area of oak woodland, probably a remnant of the vast woodlands that used to cover much of North Wales.

Head uphill beside the lovely surging river – there are lots of small waterfalls – turn left over a footbridge and continue climbing quite steeply. After passing through an area of dark, gloomy conifers, you eventually emerge from the trees to climb a ladder-stile. Keep ahead, climb two ladder-stiles in quick succession and continue up to a track. Bear right along it to where it in turn bears right; ahead there is a disused footbridge over the track. At this point turn sharp left **A** and walk along either a former railway track or the parallel path just below it. The two routes meet at Dduallt station; if on the track you go through a gate, if using the path you climb a ladder-stile. Turn left over the railway line, walk past the station buildings and at the end of the platform, turn right to re-cross the line and climb a ladder-stile. Turn left along a path which keeps roughly parallel to the line, pass under a bridge and go through two wall-gaps to reach another ladder-stile. On this part of the walk the views down the wooded Vale of

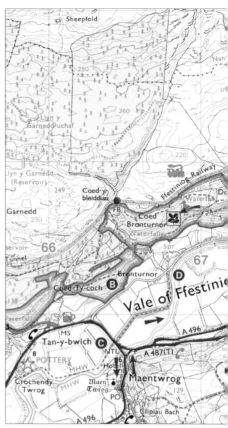

The Afon Dwyryd

Ffestiniog and over the surrounding mountains are superb and, at times, the buildings of Trawsfynydd Nuclear Power Station appear on the horizon.

Climb the stile, cross the line again, climb another ladder-stile and turn right on to a path that descends along the side of the valley to join a track in front of a house. Keep ahead along the steadily descending track – it later becomes a tarmac track – and where it does a U-bend to the left, keep ahead over a stile at a public footpath sign. Head down to cross a stream below a waterfall, continue downhill to a kissing-gate, go through, bear left and descend steeply to a concrete track. Turn right uphill, passing to the left of a house, and cross a footbridge over a stream to reach a

fork. Ignore the yellow waymark that points ahead and take the path to the left that leads to a gate. Go through and follow a path downhill through bracken – this may become overgrown during the summer – to go through a gate on to a lane **B**. Turn right to the main road and turn left along it. Just before the bridge over the Afon Dwyryd, the route turns left **C** but a brief detour into the attractive village of Maentwrog is worthwhile. Take the first turning on the right, cross the river and at a T-junction turn right through the village, built in the early 19th century by William Oakley, a local slate magnate. The spire of the Victorian church is appropriately covered in slate.

Retrace your steps over the bridge, turn right through a metal kissing-gate **C** at a public footpath sign, and walk

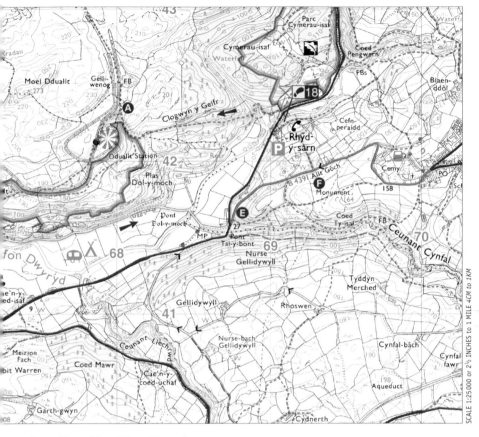

SCALE 1:25'000 or 2½ INCHES to 1 MILE 4CM to 1KM

```
0     200    400    600   800 METRES  1
                                      KILOMETRES
                                      MILES
0     200    400   600 YARDS  ½
```

along the top of an embankment. Along this stretch of the route you can enjoy the fine views looking up the wooded vale, framed by mountains and with lush riverside meadows on either side. On approaching the river the path curves left to a gate. Go through, turn right **D** and keep along a quiet, attractive lane for the next 1½ miles (2.4km) – initially beside the river, then bending right to cross it, and finally continuing by a tributary stream (Afon Cynfal) up to a road.

Turn sharp right to a junction, turn sharp left, in the Ffestiniog direction, and at a public footpath sign, turn right over a stone stile **E**. Head uphill through woodland, climb a ladder-stile,

keep ahead to emerge from the trees and go through a wall-gap to a T-junction. Turn left and head down, by a wall on the left, to climb a stile on to the road. Turn right uphill, at a public footpath sign turn left **F** through a gate and continue downhill along an enclosed path. After going through a metal gate, the path heads more steeply down to go through a metal kissing-gate at the bottom.

Cross a boggy patch and bear right to walk along the bottom edge of the field to the corner, where you head up, following the right-hand edge of the field past a waymarker. Go through a gap at the top and keep straight ahead, with a wall on your left, to a stile. Cross this and bear left onto a track. Follow this downhill to a road and turn sharp right to return to the start ●

Llanrwst, Gwydyr Forest and Trefriw

Start	Llanrwst
Distance	6 miles (9.7km)
Approximate time	3 hours
Parking	Llanrwst
Refreshments	Pubs and cafés at Llanrwst, pubs and cafés at Trefriw
Ordnance Survey maps	Landrangers 115 (Snowdon) and 116 (Denbigh & Colwyn Bay), Explorer OL17 (Snowdon)

The first and last parts of the walk are across attractive meadows bordering the River Conwy; most of the remainder is through woodland on the eastern slopes of Gwydyr Forest, from where there is a succession of fine views over the Conwy valley. Historic interest is provided by three interesting churches, a 15th-century courthouse and a 17th-century bridge. Some climbing is involved through the forest but none of it is too steep or strenuous.

The pleasant market town of Llanrwst lies on the eastern bank of the River Conwy, here spanned by a fine three-arched bridge, built in 1636 and possibly designed by Inigo Jones. On the west side of the bridge is Tu-hwnt-i'r-bont, a 15th-century former courthouse, now owned by the National Trust and used as a giftshop and tearoom. The imposing church, largely rebuilt in the 1880s, is noted for its carved rood screen and loft, and for the adjacent Gwydir Chapel, built in the 17th century as the mausoleum for the Gwynne family of Gwydir Castle. At one time the large stone coffin in it was thought to be that of Llewellyn the Great.

The walk starts in the market place in the town centre. Walk along the main road in the Betws-y-Coed direction, turn right to cross the old bridge over the River Conwy and immediately turn left **A** at a public footpath sign, along a tarmac path. Continue beside the river – a delightful stretch of riverside walking with grand views upstream – going through a metal kissing-gate and keeping ahead to a stile.

After climbing the stile, turn right along the right edge of a field up to a metal gate, go through and turn right along a road. At a sign to Gwydyr Uchaf Chapel **B**, turn sharp left up a tarmac drive and where the drive bends equally sharply to the right, keep ahead – just to the right of a bench – along a steep uphill path through trees, here entering Gwydyr Forest. The path curves left to reach a broad track; turn sharp right along it and at a fork immediately ahead, take the right-hand lower track. From this track there are attractive views through the trees to the right, over Llanrwst and the Conwy

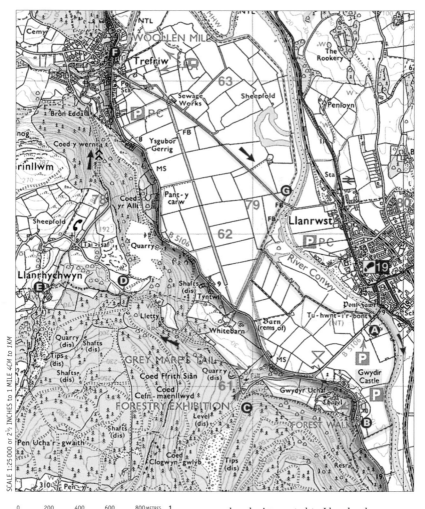

0	200	400	600	800 METRES	1	
						KILOMETRES
						MILES
0	200	400	600 YARDS	½		

valley. The track passes above Gwydyr
Uchaf Chapel to which a short detour
can be made by turning right along a
track and, where it bends right, keeping
ahead down a shady path, climbing two
stiles. Originally built for the Gwynne
family in 1604, it has a fine painted
ceiling. The home of the Gwynnes, the
much-restored Tudor mansion of
Gwydir Castle, is nearby.

Return to the main route, where the
track continues along the edge of the
forest to emerge on to a lane at a
junction **C**. Take the narrow lane

ahead, signposted to Llanrhychwyn,
cross a stream, and a ladder-stile on the
right gives access to the Grey Mare's
Tail waterfall. The lane soon starts to
head quite steeply uphill and after
³/₄ mile (1.2km), turn left **D** at a public
footpath sign, along a path to a ladder-
stile. Climb it and now comes a
particularly attractive part of the walk
as you keep ahead, first by a broken
wall on the right and later by a wire
fence on the left, through woodland.
After going through a metal gate,
continue along the right edge of a field,
then keep ahead through more trees and
bear left to go through another metal
gate. Walk along the right edge of a

field towards farm buildings and go through a metal gate to a track a few yards ahead **E**. For another brief detour, this time to Llanrhychwyn Old Church, turn left towards the farm and then turn right along a path to the church, a delightfully unspoilt, small, simple Welsh church with a whitewashed interior. Otherwise turn right along the fence-lined track which leads to a crossroads in the tiny hamlet. Keep ahead along a narrow lane, in the Trefriw direction, and there are impressive views of the houses of Trefriw ahead, clinging to the sides of the steep hillside above the valley, as the lane descends steeply into the village. At a public footpath sign on the edge of Trefriw, turn right down an enclosed path, continue downhill along a road and, where it turns right, keep ahead to cross a bridge over the Afon Crafnant. Continue along an enclosed path to a road, turn right downhill and

The River Conwy at Llanrwst

at a crossroads, turn right again down to the main road and village centre **F**.

Trefriw is noted for its woollen mill where visitors can watch the various stages in the production of tweeds and tapestries. Just to the north of the village is the Victorian spa of Trefriw Wells. Turn right to re-cross the Crafnant by Trefriw Woollen Mills and take the first turning on the left, passing a parking area. Continue along a straight, tarmac drive for just under 1 mile (1.6km) to reach a suspension bridge over the River Conwy. Do not cross it but turn right **G** over a stile and walk along the top of an embankment. Climb a stile, turn left down to climb another one, cross a footbridge over a stream and follow a path along the left edge of a series of fields and over a succession of stiles. Eventually climb a ladder-stile and turn left along an enclosed, hedge-lined track which bears right and continues to a road. Turn left and re-cross the old bridge over the river to return to the centre of Llanrwst. ●

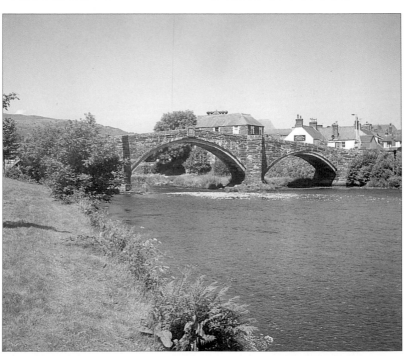

Rhaeadr Mawddach and Pistyll Cain

Start	Ganllwyd, National Trust car park at south end of the village
Distance	7 miles (11.3km)
Approximate time	3½ hours
Parking	Ganllwyd
Refreshments	None
Ordnance Survey maps	Landranger 124 (Dolgellau), Explorer OL18 (Harlech, Porthmadog & Bala)

The title of this walk uses the names of the two waterfalls that are its chief focal points and most spectacular features. Almost the whole route is through the woodlands of the vast Coed-y-Brenin Forest, an easy walk mostly along broad, clear tracks with only relatively gentle climbing. From the higher and more open parts, there are fine views over the surrounding mountains of the Rhinog and Cadair Idris ranges.

With your back to the car park, cross the road and turn right, passing the village school. Cross to the right beyond the lay-by and then fork right down the 'No Through Road' at the speed de-restriction signs. Cross the bridge over the Afon Eden **Ⓐ** and bear right, following this tarred lane past a telephone exchange and into magnificent fir-woods. At a left bend in ½ mile (800m), fork right down a wide rough lane, passing a Geology Trail board to reach and cross a long footbridge across the Mawddach. Turn left along the forestry road beyond.

In ¼ mile (400m) fork left past a gate, the route still following the gorge of the Mawddach and confirmed by yellow-topped posts. In a just over ½ mile (1km), again fork left at a junction; the roadway eventually bends sharply left, in due course emerging from the trees

to unveil a view down into the gorge and the Rhaeadr Mawddach Falls.

Only 160 yds (150m) or so past this point **Ⓑ**, fork left down a steep roadway to and across a stone river bridge. Your way is left along the roadway at the far side, passing above the Rhaeadr Mawddach. In the wooded hills up to your right is the Gwynfynnyd gold mine. Gold was first found here in 1863 but it was not until 1887 that it became fully exploited under William Pritchard Morgan, the Welsh gold king. The mine closed in 1916, reopened in the 1930s and is still being worked. The route continues to the left, heading downhill and bearing right to keep beside the River Gain near its confluence with the Mawddach. On the left is the site of the gold-mine mill. It closed a year after the mine, in 1917, was rebuilt in the 1930s but burnt down

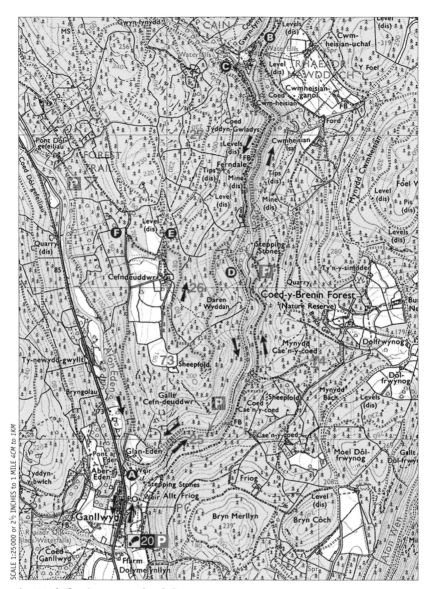

in 1935 before it was completed. Sweep left across the wide, rusty metal bridge over the Afon Gain; to your right is the spectacular Pistyll Cain, after decent rain one of the most impressive falls in Snowdonia.

Remain on the rough road, **C** eventually passing the buildings at Ferndale holiday cottages. Beyond a gateway the track becomes a tarred lane, shortly reaching the Tyddyn Gwladys forestry car park. Some 160 yds (150m) beyond this look right

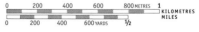

for a sharp turn back up along another forestry track **D**, this one marked by an orange cycle track sign and a blue Karrimor post. (*At this point you can choose to remain on the tarred lane back to Ganllwyd, or rise into the woods via Points* **E** *and* **F**). To reach Point **E**, follow the track around a sharp left bend, continue steadily uphill, then go round a U-bend to the right and eventually the track emerges into an open area. Here there is a white-topped post on the right but you turn sharp left **E** down to a gate. Go through, turn right, go through a metal gate and walk across open grassland, enjoying the mountain views. Go through another metal gate to a T-junction and turn left **F** along a track above the steep-sided valley of the River Eden. Cadair Idris is ahead as the track – which later becomes a tarmac track – re-enters woodland and descends, quite steeply in places, to a fork where cycle route 8 goes left. Here, remain on the tarred lane down to a cottage beside the bridge over the Afon Eden. Cross the bridge, rise to the main road and walk downhill to return to the car park. ●

The River Mawddach near Ganllwyd

Penmaenmawr and the Druid's Circle

Penmaenmawr and the Druid's Circle

Start	Penmaenmawr, by the library in town centre
Distance	4½ miles (7.2km)
Approximate time	2½ hours
Parking	Penmaenmawr, car park by library
Refreshments	Pubs and cafés at Penmaenmawr
Ordnance Survey maps	Landranger 115 (Snowdon), Explorer OL17 (Snowdon)

Because the initial climb from Penmaenmawr is steep and unrelenting, it's best to take your time and make use of the frequently occurring seats in order to enjoy the grand views over both the mountains and the coast. The route leads on to open moorland on the slopes of the Carneddau and passes the Druid's Circle, the most outstanding and atmospheric of the many prehistoric remains in this area. After a fresh and invigorating ramble across the moorland, there is a relatively easy descent back to the town.

The small coastal town of Penmaenmawr is squeezed between mountains and sea and hemmed in by the steep headlands on either side. Before the 19th century it was largely cut off by land, as travellers had to go over the top of the headlands – a hazardous journey – but the Victorians quarried away part of Penmaen Mawr and tunnelled a railway and road through between Conwy and Bangor. In the 19th century it became a popular seaside resort, much favoured by Gladstone, and has a fine sandy beach, but its heyday ended with changing tastes and the growth of foreign travel.

🖉 Turn right out of the car park and immediately right again along Yr Berllan. Take the first turning on the left – almost doubling back – then the next turning on the right and, where the road

ends, keep ahead along an enclosed, hedge-lined track. Head gently uphill to join Craiglwyd Road, turn right **Ⓐ** and at a public footpath sign to the Druid's Circle, turn left up a farm track.

Climb over a ladder-stile, pass to the left of the farm and at a wall corner, bear right and head up a grassy bank to go through a metal kissing-gate. Now comes the start of the steep and quite tiring climb on to the moorland above Penmaenmawr. After a few yards bear left and follow a clear, grassy, uphill path through some bracken. There are benches provided to enable you to take frequent rests and enjoy the superb views across the town and coast to the headland of the Great Orme. The path later bears to the right, becomes steeper and eventually turns left, crosses a concrete section laid over wet and

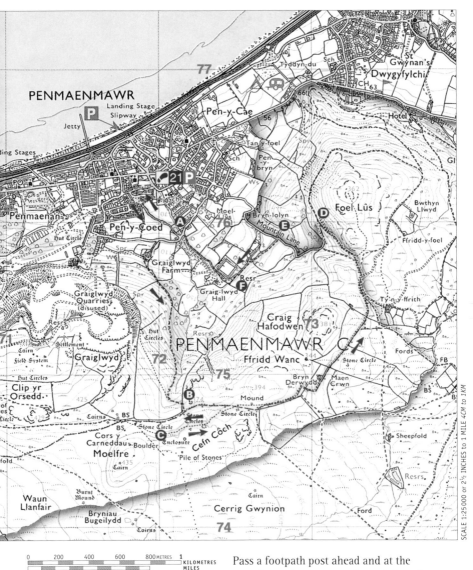

boggy ground and continues up to a metal gate.

From here there is a particularly fine view of Penmaenmawr below, cradled between the steep headlands of Penmaen Mawr (from which the town gets its name) and Penmaen-bach.

Go through the gate, turn right and follow the wall to a small stone enclosure then turn left **B** on to a track which is part of the North Wales Path.

Pass a footpath post ahead and at the next footpath post, turn sharp right and follow a clear, grassy path up to the stone circle seen ahead **C**. Although called Maeni Hirion or the Druid's Circle, it is much older than the Druids and probably dates back to the Bronze Age. There is another stone circle beyond. It enjoys a marvellously atmospheric setting up on these bare moorland slopes of the Carneddau, high above the sea.

Retrace your steps down to the track and continue along it, later keeping by

The Druid's Circle

a wall on the right. Follow the direction of a footpath post to the right, go through a metal gate, keep ahead and at the next footpath post, turn left along a beautiful tree-lined track, passing to the right of a house. In the field on the right is a standing stone.

Keep ahead along the track, going through a metal gate. Continue ahead, ignoring a metal gate and North Wales Path sign off to the right. Go through another metal gate, eventually bearing left to join a track which starts to descend. Turn sharp left in front of gateposts **D** to continue more steeply downhill – the track becomes a tarmac one. Go over a cattle-grid and, ignoring

a footpath sign, continue ahead as far as the next public footpath sign on the left **E**. Here go up steps and through a metal kissing-gate to walk along the right edge of a field, following a series of white walker marker posts. Bear right to join a lower track and look out for a ladder-stile in the wall on the right.

Climb it, continue by a fence on the right that borders a reservoir and follow the fence to the right **F** to keep along an enclosed path, between the reservoir on the right and a caravan site on the left. Go through a metal kissing-gate, turn left along a tarmac drive and at a T-junction turn left. Immediately turn right along a track **A**, here picking up the outward route, and retrace your steps to the start. ●

Penycloddiau and Moel Arthur

Start	Moel Famau Country Park, Llangwyfan car park, 1 mile (1.6km) east of Llangwyfan village
Distance	7½ miles (12.1km)
Approximate time	3½ hours
Parking	Llangwyfan car park
Refreshments	None
Ordnance Survey maps	Landranger 116 (Denbigh & Colwyn Bay), Explorer 265 (Clwydian Range)

The first and last parts of the route involve two ascents and descents as you follow Offa's Dyke Path along the ridge of the Clwydian Hills, passing the prehistoric hillforts of Penycloddiau and Moel Arthur. The remainder is along clearly defined and generally flat tracks that contour along the side of the hills, making for easy, attractive and trouble-free walking. There are some pleasant wooded stretches and continuously fine views across the broad Vale of Clwyd.

Begin by going through a gate, at the fork in front take the right-hand track and at the next fork a few yards ahead, take the right-hand, uphill path, following Offa's Dyke Path waymarks. The path runs parallel to the track and heads uphill, steeply at times, along the right edge of conifers to a stile.

Turn right over it, here crossing the outer earthworks of Penycloddiau, an Iron Age hillfort, and continue uphill across the middle of the fort. After passing a cairn, you reach the outer defences again and at this

On the shoulder of Moel Arthur

A pleasant track in the Clwydian Hills

point the views from this ridgetop track, to the right and left and ahead along the rolling Clwydian range, are magnificent. Bear right for a few yards and then turn left to continue across heathery moorland, descending to a stile. Climb it and continue downhill to a track and the next stile **Ⓐ**.

Do not climb this one but turn left on to a broad track by a wire fence on the right. Keep along this winding track for the next $2\frac{1}{2}$ miles (4km), going through several gates, passing by the edge of attractive woodland at one stage, and with glorious views across the Vale of Clwyd all the time. Finally the track bears left and keeps below conifers to reach a lane **Ⓑ**.

Bear left, follow the lane around a right-hand bend and where it bends to the left, turn right at a public bridleway

sign, along a track. This is another curving, partially wooded track which you follow through several more gates and from which there are again superb views over the vale to be enjoyed. After $1\frac{3}{4}$ miles (2.8km), you go through a metal gate on to a lane **Ⓒ**, turn left and follow the lane as far as Moel Arthur car park **Ⓓ**.

Turn left up steps, at an Offa's Dyke Path footpath post, go through a kissing-gate and head over the right shoulder of Moel Arthur, another Iron Age hillfort. Continue across heathery moorland and later descend to a stile. Climb it, descend across grass to climb another and continue more steeply downhill to the next stile. Climb that one, keep ahead to a lane and turn right to the start.　　●

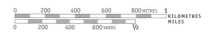

Llyn Brenig

Start	Llyn Brenig visitor centre
Distance	10 miles (16.1km)
Approximate time	4½ hours
Parking	Llyn Brenig visitor centre
Refreshments	Café at visitor centre
Ordnance Survey maps	Landranger 116 (Denbigh & Colwyn Bay), Explorer 264 (Vale of Clwyd)

Llyn Brenig is situated amidst the forests and rolling moorlands of Mynydd Hiraethog. This clear and well-waymarked circuit of the reservoir, which mainly uses a mixture of lakeside paths and tracks and forest roads, goes across meadows, over heathery moorland and through the conifer woods of Clocaenog Forest. Although a lengthy walk, the terrain is generally flat and easy, with the likelihood of a few muddy stretches, and there is a succession of fine views across the lake.

From the car park head down to the visitor centre, turn right in front of it and take the track alongside the lake. The entire circuit is regularly waymarked with walker symbols. Where the track bears right uphill, keep ahead over a stile and continue to a T-junction to the right of the dam **A**.

Turn left across the dam, at another T-junction on the far side turn left again **B** and keep beside the lake, going through two gates. After the second gate, turn right to continue through conifers and on emerging from them, go through another gate to regain the lakeshore. Shortly after going round a small inlet, you reach a circular enclosure, a Ring Cairn dating from around 2000 BC. Although in use as a cemetery, this was probably more of a ceremonial monument where friends and relatives came to grieve. There is a large tumulus (burial mound) to the right and several more in the vicinity.

Continue beside the lake, go through a gate into a car park and picnic area **C** and head gently uphill along a tarmac track, here entering Gors Maen Llwyd Nature Reserve, an area of wetland and heather moorland. At the top of a slight hill, bear left on to a path **D** that curves gradually left across the moorland, keeping roughly parallel to a road on the right. The path is not always clear on the ground but there are regular waymarked posts.

The route continues across grassland and, after climbing some steps, heads once more across heathery moorland. Look out for where a footpath post directs you to turn right and on reaching a track, turn left **E** along it, gently ascending and then descending to go through a gate on the edge of conifer woodland. The rest of the walk

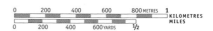

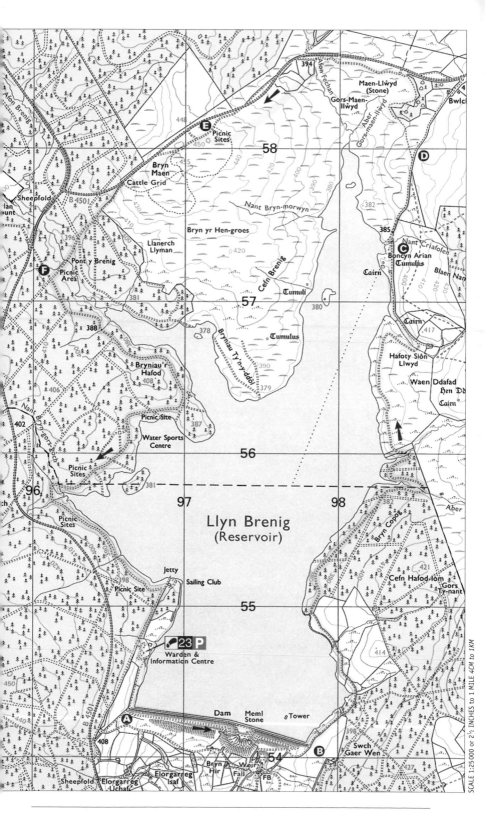

LLYN BRENIG ● 71

is through conifers, part of the vast Clocaenog Forest, with Llyn Brenig sometimes visible on the left.

Walk along a track to join a forest road at a U-bend and keep along it, crossing a stream (Afon Brenig) and passing through another picnic area.

Follow the road to the left **F**, continue along it, rounding several bends as you follow the contours of the lakeshore, and at a fork take the left-hand road which leads back to the start. ●

Llyn Brenig and the Ring Cairn

Llangollen, Castell Dinas Bran and Valle Crucis Abbey

Start	Llangollen
Distance	8½ miles (13.7km)
Approximate time	5 hours
Parking	Llangollen
Refreshments	Pubs and cafés at Llangollen
Ordnance Survey maps	Landrangers 117 (Chester & Wrexham) and 125 (Bala & Lake Vymwy), Explorers 255 (Llangollen & Berwyn) and 256 (Wrexham)

This is one of the great classic walks of North Wales with stunning views of the Vale of Llangollen and the Berwyn Mountains, plus plenty of scenic variety and considerable historic interest. Initially there is a steep climb to the scanty remains of Castell Dinas Bran, a superb viewpoint above Llangollen, followed by a rather easier descent and a lovely walk below the limestone cliffs of Eglwyseg, curving round to the substantial ruins of Valle Crucis Abbey. The route continues over Velvet Hill to the Horseshoe Falls on the River Dee, and the final stretch is a relaxing stroll through the valley along the towpath of the Shropshire Union Canal.

Surrounded by hills and famed as the venue for the annual International Musical Eisteddfod, Llangollen is an excellent touring and walking centre. It lies on the banks of the River Dee, spanned by a 14th-century bridge which is one of the 'Seven Wonders of Wales'. Nearby is the old church of St Collen from which the town gets its name. The black and white house of Plas Newydd and its gardens, home of the Ladies of Llangollen, is just to the south. The two ladies, Eleanor Butler and Sarah Ponsonby, eloped here in the early 19th century and over the years

entertained many of the leading political and literary figures of the time, including the Duke of Wellington, William Wordsworth and Sir Walter Scott. Among Llangollen's other attractions are a ride on the steam-hauled Llangollen Railway, boat trips, some horse-drawn, along the banks of the Shropshire Union Canal, and a visit to ECTARC, the European Centre for Traditional and Regional Cultures.

🖉 The walk begins at the south end of Llangollen Bridge. Cross the bridge, turn right and then turn left up Wharf Hill, crossing the canal bridge, to reach

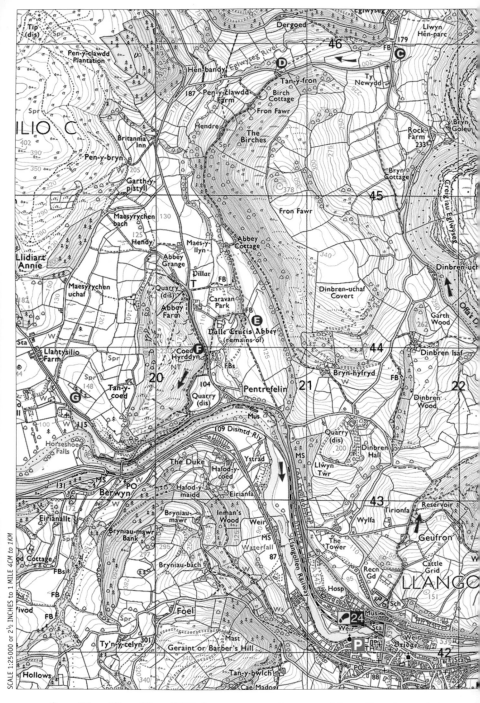

The first part of the walk to the castle is all uphill. Cross a track by school buildings, continue along a steadily ascending path and, after passing through a kissing-gate, the going becomes steeper as you keep along the

a T-junction. Go up the steps ahead, at a public footpath sign to Castell Dinas Bran, and walk along an enclosed path.

SCALE 1:25000 or 2½ INCHES to 1 MILE 4CM to 1KM

right edge of a field to another kissing-gate. Go through, continue along a track, keep ahead at a crossroads, go through a kissing-gate and bear right. The route continues across a flat, grassy plateau before the final, steep, zigzag pull up to the summit of the conical hill crowned by the scanty remains of Castell Dinas Bran **Ⓐ**. There was originally a prehistoric hillfort on the site but the present ruins are those of a 13th-century castle established by the princes of Powys. The magnificent views more than compensate for the effort; they include the Berwyn Mountains, Eglwyseg Cliffs and Llangollen, and extend along the Dee valley to the Pontcysyllte Aqueduct and across the English border into Shropshire.

Continue past the castle, following a series of waymarked posts which lead down to a stile at a fence corner. Climb it, follow a winding path steeply downhill and climb a stile on to a track. Turn left, go through a metal gate and turn left again along a narrow lane **Ⓑ**, here joining Offa's Dyke Path. Keep along this lane below the formidable-looking Eglwyseg Cliffs for 1¼ miles (2km) and about 100 yards (91m) after a lane joins from the left, bear left, at a public footpath sign, along a grassy track to a stile.

Climb it, keep ahead by a hedge-bank on the right, climb another stile and head across a field, bearing left to climb a waymarked stile in the far left corner. Cross a footbridge over a stream, continue along the left edge of a field and just before reaching the corner, bear right and head across to a footpath post. Go through a gap in a line of trees, keep by a wire fence on the left and go through a metal gate to rejoin the lane.

Bear left, take the first turning on the left **Ⓒ** and after ½ mile (0.8km) – where the lane descends to a farm and bends right – bear left on to a track, at a public footpath sign to Valle Crucis Abbey **Ⓓ**. The track undulates through the Eglwyseg valley below sloping woodland on the left, and at a fork take the right-hand track which descends and turns right to a ladder-stile. Climb it, keep ahead and in front of a cottage turn left over another ladder-stile. Walk along the right edge of a field, climb a stile and a few yards ahead, turn right **Ⓔ** and descend a flight of steps to a footbridge over the River Eglwyseg. Cross it, continue through a caravan site, picking up a track, and go through a gate on to a tarmac drive. To the left are the beautiful ruins of Valle Crucis Abbey, the finest in North Wales, a Cistercian monastery founded in 1201 by the princes of Powys. Much of the church survives, including the fine west front and east end. Among the other buildings grouped around the cloister, the elegantly vaulted chapter house is

Valle Crucis Abbey

particularly outstanding. Walk along the drive, passing in front of the abbey, and where it bears left, keep ahead through a kissing-gate, at a public footpath sign to Velvet Hill, and head diagonally across a field. Go through a kissing-gate in the far corner, turn left along a road and at another public footpath sign to Velvet Hill, turn right **F** and head uphill to a stile. Climb over it, continue steeply uphill to a footpath post and turn left on to a path that contours along the side of the hill, curving right and descending between some trees and bracken to a stile. Climb it, continue through some trees and descend steps to emerge on to a road at a junction.

Turn right, in the Llantysilio and Rhewl direction, and below on the left are fine views of the Horseshoe Falls, Llantysilio church and the bend in the River Dee. At a public footpath sign 'Horseshoe Falls, Chain Bridge, Llangollen', turn sharp left **G** down a track and go through a metal kissing-gate to the left of the lych-gate to Llantysilio's attractive 15th-century church. Descend steps, continue down to the river and go through a metal gate to join a riverside path. Walk beside the Horseshoe Falls and turn right through another metal gate. The falls feed the Llangollen branch of the Shropshire Union Canal which begins here.

Turn left on to the canal towpath for a relaxing 2-mile (3.2km) walk back to Llangollen. It is a most attractive finale, with the River Dee on your right as you walk along, and you pass under several bridges. Just before reaching Llangollen Wharf, leave the towpath by keeping ahead down a tarmac path which curves right to reach a road. Turn left and then right over the bridge to return to the starting point. ●

Cilcain and Moel Famau

Start	Loggerheads Country Park
Distance	8 miles (12.9km)
Approximate time	5 hours
Parking	Loggerheads Country Park
Refreshments	Café at Country Park, pub at Loggerheads, pub at Cilcain
Ordnance Survey maps	Landranger 116 (Denbigh & Colwyn Bay), Explorer 265 (Clwydian Range)

This lengthy and highly enjoyable walk includes an ascent of Moel Famau, at 1818 feet (554m) the highest point on the Clwydian Hills and a magnificent viewpoint. The first part of the route is along a most attractive path, the Leete Path, which runs along the side of the wooded Alyn valley. It continues into Cilcain and descends from the village, after which comes the long, steady and, towards the end, steep climb across open moorland to the summit of Moel Famau. The descent, through the conifers of Clwyd Forest is reasonably easy and straightforward.

It is thought that the name 'Logger-heads' may have originated from a lengthy feud in the 18th century between two local landowners over estate boundaries and mineral rights.

✎ Start by walking in front of the information centre and café, cross a bridge over the River Alyn and turn left along a riverside path. Follow the path through woodland and go through a kissing-gate at a sign for 'Leete Walk'. Continue along a most attractive path that keeps above the river, through trees and beside the face of limestone cliffs. In summer the Alyn dries up and flows underground in places, a common feature of limestone country. The Leete Walk gets its name from a channel built in 1823 to carry water from the river – bypassing the dry sections – to power water wheels. The path follows the route of this channel.

Later the path widens into a track – where this becomes a tarmac one and heads uphill, bear left off it, at a public footpath sign 'Leete Path, Cilcain', to continue along a path through the trees. At a fork take the left-hand lower path, cross a bridge over the spectacular Devil's Gorge, the remains of a calcite

Cilcain church

mine, and eventually the path emerges on to a road **A**. Turn sharp left downhill, cross the river, head up and where the road bends right, keep ahead, at a public footpath sign to Pentre, along a narrow, enclosed path above the wooded valley of Nant Gain. Climb a stile and continue along the left edge of a succession of fields and over a series of stiles, keeping along the top edge of steeply sloping woodland all the time. Turn left over a stile in a fence, turn right and continue along the top inside edge of the woodland to a stile. Climb it, head down to join another path and turn right uphill to a lane **B**. Turn right, continue uphill into Cilcain and in front of the White Horse turn left, passing to the right of the church. This mainly 14th- and 15th-century building is noted for its complex and richly decorated nave roof. Too elaborate for a small village church, it is believed to have been brought here from a larger church, perhaps a dissolved abbey, during the Reformation, but its exact origins are a mystery. After passing the church, turn left again **C** along a lane that heads downhill. At a sharp left bend, go through a metal gate opposite **D** and, at a public footpath sign a few yards ahead, turn right over a stone stile. Walk along the left edge of two fields, climbing a stile, and in the corner of the second one climb another stile and continue along a gently ascending hedge-lined track. Climb a stile, continue steadily uphill, go through a gate and keep ahead through trees and bracken, later climbing more steeply across open, heathery moorland to a crossroads on the edge of a conifer plantation. Continue along the right edge of the conifers up to the Jubilee Tower on the summit of Moel Famau **E** to enjoy the magnificent and extensive view over the Vale of Clwyd. The rather

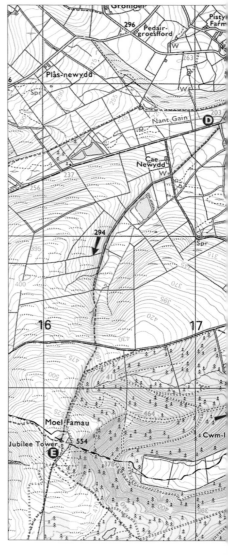

squat tower, built in 1810 to commemorate George III's Golden Jubilee, was originally much higher but was partially destroyed by a severe storm in 1862.

From the tower, turn left across to the triangulation pillar and head towards two stiles, side by side, at which point there is a public footpath sign to Loggerheads. Climb one of the stiles and take the track ahead which descends, quite steeply at times, between the bracken and conifers of Clwyd Forest. Cross a forest road, continue downhill and at the bottom

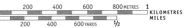

SCALE 1:25 000 or 2½ INCHES to 1 MILE 4CM to 1KM

climb a stile on to a track **F**. Turn right, climb another stile, ford a stream and turn left along the left edge of a field, alongside the stream, as far as a waymarked post. Turn half-right, walk across the field to the next waymarked post and continue past it, by the left edge of the field, to cross a footbridge over a stream.

At a footpath post bear left up to the next one and bear left again, by a wire fence bordering steeply sloping woodland on the right, to a ladder-stile. Climb it, continue along the bottom inside edge of the conifers to climb

another and head across a field corner to the next stile. Climb that one, turn left along a track to a T-junction and turn right along the left edge of a field. Go through a gap, keep along the right edge of the next field, climb a stile and keep ahead along a track, by a stream on the left, to a metal gate. Go through, turn right **G** along a lane and take the first turning on the left. Follow the lane for ½ mile (0.8km) back to Loggerheads Country Park.

●

Bwlch Maen Gwynedd

Start	Llandrillo
Distance	9½ miles (15.3km)
Approximate time	5 hours
Parking	Llandrillo
Refreshments	None
Ordnance Survey maps	Landranger 125 (Bala & Lake Vyrnwy), Explorer 255 (Llangollen & Berwyn)

The walk leads through austere and lonely terrain into the heart of the Berwyn Mountains to Bwlch Maen Gwynedd, a gap in the long ridge between Cadair Bronwen and Cadair Berwyn, two of the highest peaks in the range. Bwlch Maen Gwynedd itself is at 2290 feet (698m) and from it the views, along the ridge and down into the valleys on both sides, are awe-inspiring. On the outward route some sections of the path are indistinct and you have to avoid a boggy area. The return is along a much clearer and easier track, but this walk does involve rough walking across open moorland and hillside and should not be attempted in bad weather, especially misty conditions, unless you are an experienced hill walker able to navigate by using a compass.

Llandrillo is attractively situated on the Afon Ceidiog, a tributary of the River Dee, and from the bridge there is a fine view of the tower and spire of the church rising above the village.

🖉 Start by turning left out of the car park and turn right along a path that runs along the right edge of the library to a stile. Climb it, continue along an enclosed path to climb another and keep ahead along the right edge of a field. At a hedge corner turn left, continue across the field and climb a stile on to a tarmac track **A**.

Turn right, go through a gate and walk steadily uphill, passing to the left of a house (Llechwedd), to a metal gate on the edge of woodland. Go through, continue along the right edge of the wood, go through another metal gate

and on meeting another track, keep along it to a fork. Take the left-hand uphill track, go through a metal gate to emerge from the trees and at the next fork, take the right-hand lower track. The track continues steadily uphill to a metal gate. Go through and ahead are the bare, open slopes of the Berwyns.

At a junction of tracks **B** keep ahead through another metal gate, at a public bridleway sign to Craig Berwyn, and continue along a track which may be muddy and waterlogged in places. The track descends to a stream (Clochnant) but at this stage it is important to bear left away from the stream in order to avoid a marshy area ahead, Gwern Wynodl. The path tends to peter out here but aim for the higher, drier, heathery moorland to the left, later bearing right

Llandrillo and the Dee Valley

back towards the stream and making for the distinct landmark of a small, rectangular conifer wood clearly seen ahead. As you head towards it, a definite path appears again and you continue to a metal gate. Go through, keep ahead, passing along the right edge of the conifer wood, ford a stream and continue along a clear and obvious path that climbs gently above Clochnant. Ahead is an impressive view looking towards the head of the valley and the Berwyn ridge. At a fork take the right-hand lower path, ford a tributary stream and continue uphill. The path briefly becomes soggy and indistinct again and

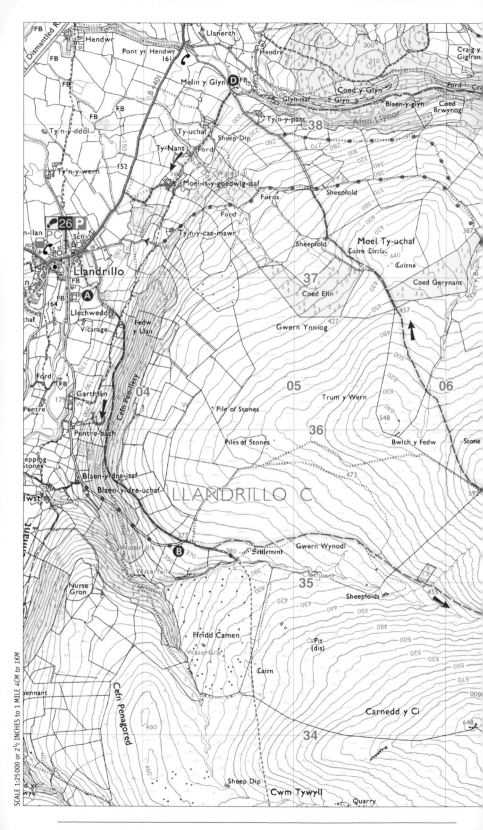

SCALE 1:25000 or 2½ INCHES to 1 MILE 4CM to 1KM

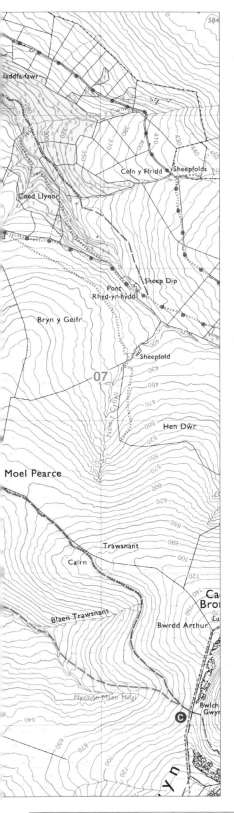

this is quite a tiring part of the walk, but you eventually reach a metal gate at the top of the pass, Bwlch Maen Gwynedd, 2290ft (698m) high **C**. Go through and keep ahead a few yards to enjoy a magnificent view: to the right along the Berwyn ridge to Cadair Berwyn, to the left along the ridge to Cadair Bronwen, behind to the Dee valley, and ahead along the steep-sided, sweeping, curving valley of Cwm Maen Gwynedd. Turn back through the gate, retrace your steps for about 100 yards (91m) to a fork – probably not noticed on the way up – and take the right-hand path which can be seen heading up over the slopes in front. The path descends initially, then continues gently up, later bearing right and curving left above the head of Blaen Trawsnant. From here there is a superb view to the left of Cadair Berwyn. Continue gently up over Moel Pearce along what has become an undulating track, joining and keeping by a wire fence on the right, and on arriving at two metal gates, go through the right-hand one. The track soon bears right away from a wire fence on the left and you follow it as it winds steadily downhill, passing along the left edge of a conifer wood (Coed Gerynant) and going through a succession of metal gates. Look out for a stone circle on the hill to the right just after the conifer wood, and all the way there are imposing views ahead of the Dee valley. Again, when confronted with two metal gates, bear right to go through the right-hand one. After the next gate, the track – now a tarmac one and enclosed – descends more steeply. Pass through several more gates to reach a road just to the left of a bridge over the Afon Llynor **D**, turn left and follow it for 1 mile (1.6km) back to Llandrillo. ●

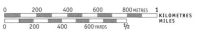

Carnedd Dafydd

Start	Ogwen, at western end of Llyn Ogwen. Shorter version starts at the eastern end of the lake
Distance	7 miles (11.3km) Shorter version 5½ miles (8.9km)
Approximate time	6 hours (5 hours for shorter version)
Parking	Ogwen. For shorter walk there are plenty of lay-bys alongside and beyond eastern end of the lake
Refreshments	Kiosk at Ogwen
Ordnance Survey maps	Landranger 115 (Snowdon), Explorer OL17 (Snowdon)

At 3423 feet (1043m) Carnedd Dafydd is one of the highest peaks in the Carneddau range and a magnificent viewpoint. After an initial walk, rocky and wet in places, along the north shore of Llyn Ogwen, there follows a fairly steep climb beside the Afon Lloer. The route then curves left and continues more steeply uphill, with some rough scrambling, to the 3211-ft (978m) summit of Pen yr Ole Wen. From there an easy ridge path leads on to Carnedd Dafydd. Because of the difficult, very steep, unstable and potentially dangerous descent down the south face of Pen yr Ole Wen to Ogwen, it is advisable to return by the same route, taking care where scrambling is required. The shorter version omits the walk beside Llyn Ogwen.

This is an enjoyable but quite challenging walk and should never be attempted in bad weather or misty conditions, especially in winter, unless you are experienced, can navigate with a compass, and equipped for mountain walking in such conditions.

🖉 Turn right out of the car park to the main road, turn left and just after crossing the bridge over the River Ogwen, turn right over a stile **A**, at a public footpath sign. Continue along a path which is rocky, badly drained and quite difficult at times, initially beside the river and later by Llyn Ogwen, to a ladder-stile. Climb it, keep ahead to climb another and continue across rocky terrain. Bear left uphill – there is no visible path – and later keep parallel to and above the lake, making for a

ladder-stile in a wire fence. Climb it, keep ahead to pass through a wall-gap and at a footpath post, bear slightly left up to another ladder-stile. Climb it, cross a footbridge over the Afon Lloer, pass two more footpath posts and at the second one, turn left uphill **B**.

At this point the shorter route joins the full walk. If starting from the east end of Llyn Ogwen, turn along a track at a public footpath sign in a group of conifers just beyond the lake. Cross a bridge over a stream, climb a ladder-

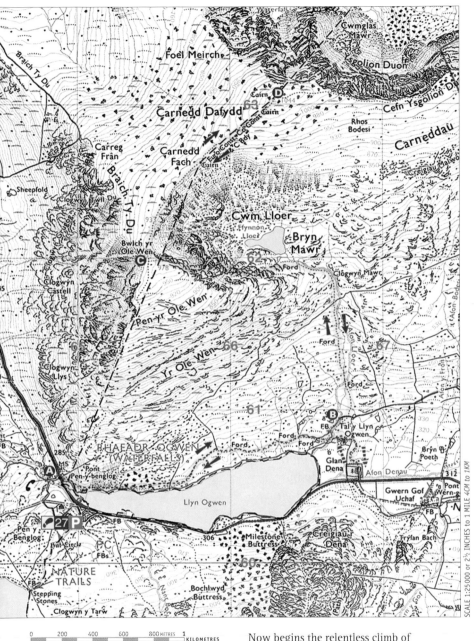

0   200   400   600   800 METRES 1
                                          KILOMETRES
                                          MILES
0   200   400   600 YARDS   ½

stile and the track winds round to a
gate. Do not go through this gate but
turn right uphill alongside a wall and
climb a ladder-stile in that wall. Head
across to a footpath post and turn right
uphill **B**.

Now begins the relentless climb of
Pen yr Ole Wen. Head uphill across
some soft and marshy ground, ford the
Afon Lloer and continue alongside its
west bank. After negotiating some rocks
– a short scramble here – ascend more
steeply to a ladder-stile. Climb it, later
curving left and continuing up along a
less obvious path, although there are

some cairns to indicate the way. The final part of the climb to the summit cairn on Pen yr Ole Wen is quite tiring and involves some rough but not hazardous scrambling; the small lake seen below the crags is Ffynnon Lloer. At the summit the splendid 360° views include the Menai Strait, Anglesey, Snowdon, Tryfan, the Glyders and the long ridge leading to Carnedd Dafydd and on to Carnedd Llewelyn. Continue past the cairn, descending slightly, and turn right **C** to follow the gently ascending, rocky ridge path to the cairn on the summit of Carnedd Dafydd, **D** just under a mile (1.6km) away and another magnificent viewpoint. From here retrace your steps back to either of the two starting points, enjoying more superb views of Tryfan, Snowdon and the Glyders and taking care on the steepest parts of the long descent. ●

Llyn Ogwen

Snowdon via the Watkin Path

Start	Pont Bethania car park, on A498 between Llyn Dinas and Llyn Gwynant
Distance	9 miles (14.5km)
Approximate time	7 hours
Parking	Pont Bethania
Refreshments	Café at Snowdon summit station (restricted opening)
Ordnance Survey maps	Landranger 115 (Snowdon), ExplorerOL17 (Snowdon)

Of the various alternative routes to the summit of Snowdon, the Watkin Path is one of the longest, but also arguably the most attractive. It is also relatively easy, but nevertheless an ascent of Snowdon must never be underestimated. A long, steady climb along a well-constructed path, passing a series of waterfalls and the remains of abandoned quarries, leads to a final scramble on to the summit ridge. From here it is a short, level walk to the 3560 feet (1085m) summit, the highest point in Britain south of the Scottish Highlands. It is a tremendously exhilarating and satisfying feeling to conquer Snowdon and enjoy what, on a clear day, are the necessarily extensive and magnificent views. The descent, also long and steady rather than steep, is a superb ridge walk, later curving through Cwm Llan to rejoin the Watkin Path.
It must be emphasised that on no account should this walk be attempted in bad weather or during the winter months, unless you are experienced in such conditions, able to navigate by using a compass and possess the right clothing, footwear and equipment.

From the car park cross the road, go through a metal gate, at a public footpath sign, and turn right along a tarmac track. At a fork, take the left-hand rough track and follow it steadily uphill, passing through several gates and keeping by the cascading Afon Cwm Llan all the while.

Cross a footbridge over the stream **A** and continue steadily uphill, passing the Gladstone Rock. At the age of 84, William Gladstone made a speech here at the opening of the Watkin Path in 1892. Soon the ascent becomes steeper, the views become more magnificent and a series of cairns marks the way. Finally you climb a steep, zigzag path – not always clearly defined – which involves some modest scrambling, to emerge on to a ridge by a large rock **B**.

SCALE 1:25000 or 2½ INCHES to 1 MILE 4CM to 1KM

0	200	400	600	800 METRES	1

KILOMETRES
MILES

0	200	400	600 YARDS	½

Turn right for the short distance to the summit station and café, and beyond that the summit cairn itself **C**.

The views are, of course, magnificent and extend over the rest of Snowdonia and much of North Wales. In exceptionally clear conditions they can embrace the Wicklow Mountains in Ireland, the Isle of Man and some of the higher Lake District peaks. The Snowdon Mountain Railway, a great triumph of Victorian engineering, is the only rack-and-pinion railway in Britain and was opened to passenger traffic in 1896. The journey from Llanberis to the summit of Snowdon is about 5 miles (8km) long, with an average gradient of 1 in 7.

From the summit retrace your steps to where you joined the ridge **B** and continue along the ridge path. In clear weather the Watkin Path can be seen over to the left and even the starting point in the Nantgwynant valley is visible far below. At a fork take the left-hand uphill path which later descends – a winding, rocky and quite difficult descent in places – to a ladder-stile.

Heading up the Watkin Path on the ascent of Yr Wyddfa – Snowdon itself

Climb it, continue downhill into a col and follow the path to the left to go through a wall-gap.

Now the going becomes easier as you continue along a grassy path through Cwm Llan to join an old tramway built to serve the copper mines in the area. Walk along this track and after passing between rocks, turn left **D** on to a path which heads down and curves right to join the outward route just to the right of a bridge over Afon Cwm Llan **A**. At a T-junction turn right on to the Watkin Path and retrace your steps to the start, enjoying the grand views to the left of Llyn Gwynant on this final leg. ●

Further Information

The National Parks and Countryside Recreation

Ten National Parks were created in England and Wales as a result of an Act of Parliament in 1949. In addition to these, there are numerous specially designated Areas of Outstanding Natural Beauty, Country and Regional Parks, Sites of Special Scientific Interest and picnic areas scattered throughout England, Wales and Scotland, all of which share the twin aims of preservation of the countryside and public accessibility and enjoyment.

John Dower, whose report in 1945 created their framework, defined a National Park as 'an extensive area of beautiful and relatively wild country in which, for the nation's benefit and by appropriate national decision and action, (a) the characteristic landscape beauty is strictly preserved, (b) access and facilities for public open-air enjoyment are amply provided, (c) wildlife and buildings and places of architectural and historic interest are suitably protected, while (d) established farming use is effectively maintained'.

Proposals for the creation of areas of protected countryside were first made before World War I, but nothing was done. The growing demand for access to open country and the reluctance of landowners – particularly those who owned large expanses of uncultivated moorland – to grant it led to a number of ugly incidents, in particular the mass trespass in the Peak District in 1932, when ramblers and gamekeepers came to blows and some trespassers received stiff prison sentences.

It was after World War II that calls for countryside conservation and access came to fruition in parliament. The National Parks and Countryside Act of 1949 provided for the designation and preservation of areas both of great scenic beauty and of particular wildlife and scientific interest throughout Britain. More specifically it provided for the creation of National Parks in England and Wales. Scotland was excluded because, with greater areas of open space and a smaller population, there were fewer pressures on the Scottish countryside.

A National Parks Commission, a forerunner of the Countryside Commission, was set up, and over the next eight years ten areas were designated as parks; seven in England (Northumberland, Lake District, North York Moors, Yorkshire Dales, Peak District, Exmoor and Dartmoor) and three in Wales (Snowdonia, Brecon Beacons and Pembrokeshire Coast). In 1989 the Norfolk and Suffolk Broads were added to the list. At the same time the Commission was also given the responsibility for designating other smaller areas of high recreational and scenic qualities (Areas of Outstanding Natural Beauty), plus the power to propose and develop long-distance footpaths, now called National Trails.

The authorities who administer the individual National Parks have the very difficult task of reconciling the interests of the people who live and earn their living within them with those of visitors. National Parks are not living museums and there is pressure to exploit the resources of the area, through more intensive farming, or through increased quarrying and forestry, extraction of minerals or the construction of reservoirs.

In the end it all comes down to a question of balance – between conservation and 'sensitive development'. On the one hand there is a responsibility to preserve the natural beauty of the National Parks and to promote their enjoyment by the public, and on the other, the needs and well-being of the people living and working in them have to be borne in mind.

The National Trust

Anyone who likes visiting places of natural beauty and/or historic interest has cause to be grateful to the National Trust. Without it, many such places would probably have vanished by now.

It was in response to the pressures on the countryside posed by the relentless march of Victorian industrialisation that the trust was set up in 1895. Its founders, inspired by the common goals of protecting and conserving Britain's national heritage and widening public access to it, were Sir Robert Hunter, Octavia Hill and Canon Rawnsley: respectively a solicitor, a social reformer and a clergyman. The latter was particularly influential. As a canon of Carlisle Cathedral and vicar of Crosthwaite (near Keswick), he was concerned about threats to the Lake District and had already been active in protecting footpaths and promoting public access to open countryside. After the flooding of Thirlmere in 1879 to create a large reservoir, he became increasingly convinced that the only effective way to guarantee protection was outright ownership of land.

The purpose of the National Trust is to preserve areas of natural beauty and sites of historic interest by acquisition, holding them in trust for the nation and making them available for public access and enjoyment. Some of its properties have been acquired through purchase, but many have been donated. Nowadays it is not only one of the biggest landowners in the country, but also one of the most active conservation charities, protecting 581,113 acres (253,176 ha) of land, including 555 miles (892km) of coastline, and over 300 historic properties in England, Wales and Northern Ireland. (There is a separate National Trust for Scotland, which was set up in 1931.)

Furthermore, once a piece of land has come under National Trust ownership, it is difficult for its status to be altered. As a result of parliamentary legislation in 1907, the Trust was given the right to declare its property inalienable, so ensuring that in any subsequent dispute it can appeal directly to parliament.

As it works towards its dual aims of conserving areas of attractive countryside and encouraging greater public access (not easy to reconcile in this age of mass tourism), the Trust provides an excellent service for walkers by creating new concessionary paths and waymarked trails, maintaining stiles and foot bridges and combating the ever-increasing problem of footpath erosion.

For details of membership, contact the National Trust at one of the addresses on page 95.

 ### The Ramblers' Association

No organisation works more actively to protect and extend the rights and interests of walkers in the countryside than the Ramblers' Association. Its aims are clear: to foster a greater knowledge, love and care of the countryside; to assist in the protection and enhancement of public rights of way

and areas of natural beauty; to work for greater public access to the countryside; and to encourage more people to take up rambling as a healthy, recreational leisure activity.

It was founded in 1935 when, following the setting up of a National Council of Ramblers' Federations in 1931, a number of federations earlier formed in London, Manchester, the Midlands and elsewhere came together to create a more effective pressure group, to deal with such problems as the disappearance and obstruction of footpaths, the prevention of access to open mountain and moorland and increasing hostility from landowners. This was the era of the mass trespasses, when there were sometimes violent confrontations between ramblers and gamekeepers, especially on the moorlands of the Peak District.

Since then the Ramblers' Association has played an influential role in preserving and developing the national footpath network, supporting the creation of national parks and encouraging the designation and waymarking of long-distance routes.

Our freedom to walk in the countryside is precarious and requires constant vigilance. As well as the perennial problems of footpaths being illegally obstructed, disappearing through lack of use or extinguished by housing or road construction, new dangers can spring up at any time.

It is to meet such problems and dangers that the Ramblers' Association exists and represents the interests of all walkers. The address to write to for information on the Ramblers' Association and how to become a member is given on page 95.

Caergwrle nestling below Hope Mountain

*Walkers and
the Law*

The average walker in a national park or other popular walking area, armed with the appropriate Ordnance Survey map, reinforced perhaps by a guidebook giving detailed walking instructions, is unlikely to run into legal difficulties, but it is useful to know something about the law relating to public rights of way. The right to walk over certain parts of the countryside has developed over a long period, and how such rights came into being is a complex subject, too lengthy to be discussed here. The following comments are intended simply as a helpful guide, backed up by the Countryside Access Charter, a concise summary of walkers' rights and obligations drawn up by the Countryside Commission.

Basically there are two main kinds of public rights of way: footpaths (for walkers only) and bridleways (for walkers, riders on horseback and pedal cyclists). Footpaths and bridleways are shown by broken green lines on Ordnance Survey Pathfinder and Outdoor Leisure maps and broken red lines on Land-ranger maps. There is also a third category, called byways: chiefly broad tracks (green lanes) or farm roads, which walkers, riders and cyclists have to share, usually only occasionally, with motor vehicles. Many of these public paths have been in existence for hundreds of years and some even originated as prehistoric trackways and have been in constant use for well over 2000 years. Ways known as RUPPs (roads used as public paths) still appear on some maps. The legal definition of such byways is ambiguous and they are gradually being reclassified as footpaths, bridleways or byways.

The term 'right of way' means exactly what it says. It gives right of passage over what, in the vast majority of cases, is private land, and you are required to keep to the line of the path and not stray to either side. If you inadvertently wander off the right of way – either because of faulty map-reading or because the route is not clearly indicated on the ground – you are technically trespassing and the wisest course is to ask the nearest available person (farmer or fellow walker) to direct you back to the correct route. There are stories about unpleasant confrontations between walkers and farmers at times, but in general most farmers are co-operative when responding to a genuine and polite request for assistance in route-finding.

 Glossary of Welsh Words

This list gives some of the more common elements in Welsh place-names, which will allow readers to understand otherwise meaningless words and appreciate the relationship between place-names and landscape features. Place-names often have variant spellings, and the more common of these are given here.

aber	estuary, confluence	foel, moel	rounded hill
afon	river	glyn	glen
bach, fach	small	hen	old
bont, pont	bridge	llan, eglwys	church
bryn	mound, hill	llyn	lake
bwlch	pass	maen	stone
caer	fort	mawr, fawr	big
capel	chapel	moel, foel	rounded hill
carn, carnedd	cairn	morfa	sea marsh
castell	castle	mynydd	mountain
ceunant	gorge, ravine	nant	brook
coed	wood	newydd	new
craig	crag	pair	cauldron
crib	narrow ridge	pen	head, top
cwm	valley	pont, bont	bridge
drws	doors, gap (pass)	pwll	pool
dyffryn	valley	rhaedr	waterfall
eglwys, llan	church	sarn	causeway
fach, bach	small	traeth	beach, shore
fawr, mawr	big	twll	hole
ffordd	road	ynys	island

Countryside Access Charter

Your rights of way are:

- public footpaths – on foot only. Sometimes waymarked in yellow
- bridleways – on foot, horseback and pedal cycle. Sometimes waymarked in blue
- byways (usually old roads), most 'roads used as public paths' and, of course, public roads – all traffic has the right of way

Use maps, signs and waymarks to check rights of way. Ordnance Survey Explorer and Landranger maps show most public rights of way

On rights of way you can:

- take a pram, pushchair or wheelchair if practicable
- take a dog (on a lead or under close control)
- take a short route round an illegal obstruction or remove it sufficiently to get past

You have a right to go for recreation to:

- public parks and open spaces – on foot
- most commons near older towns and cities – on foot and sometimes on horseback
- private land where the owner has a formal agreement with the local authority

In addition you can use the following by local or established custom or consent, but ask for advice if you are unsure:

- many areas of open country, such as moorland, fell and coastal areas, especially those in the care of the National Trust, and some commons
- some woods and forests, especially those owned by the Forestry Commission
- country parks and picnic sites
- most beaches
- canal towpaths
- some private paths and tracks Consent sometimes extends to horse-riding and cycling

For your information:

- county councils and London boroughs maintain and record rights of way, and register commons
- obstructions, dangerous animals, harassment and misleading signs on rights of way are illegal and you should report them to the county council
- paths across fields can be ploughed, but must normally be reinstated within two weeks
- landowners can require you to leave land to which you have no right of access
- motor vehicles are normally permitted only on roads, byways and some 'roads used as public paths'

Obstructions can sometimes be a problem and probably the most common of these is where a path across a field has been ploughed up. It is legal for a farmer to plough up a path provided that he restores it within two weeks, barring exceptionally bad weather. This does not always happen and here the walker is presented with a dilemma: to follow the line of the path, even if this inevitably means treading on crops, or to walk around the edge of the field. The latter course of action often seems the best but this means that you would be trespassing and not keeping to the exact line of the path. In the case of other obstructions which may block a path (illegal fences and locked gates etc), common sense has to be used in order to negotiate them by the easiest method – detour or removal. You should only ever remove as much as is necessary to get through, and if you can easily go round the

obstruction without causing any damage, then you should do so. If you have any problems negotiating rights of way, you should report the matter to the rights of way department of the relevant council, which will take whatever action is required with the landowner concerned.

Apart from rights of way enshrined by law, there are a number of other paths available to walkers. Permissive or concessionary paths have been created where a landowner has given permission for the public to use a particular route across his land. The main problem with these is that, as they have been granted as a concession, there is no legal right to use them and therefore they can be extinguished at any time. In practice, many of these concessionary routes have been established on land owned either by large public bodies such as the Forestry Commission, or by a private one, such as the

Overlooking Penmaenmawr

National Trust, and as these mainly encourage walkers to use their paths, they are unlikely to be closed unless a change of ownership occurs.

Walkers also have free access to country parks (except where requested to keep away from certain areas for ecological reasons, e.g. wildlife protection, woodland regeneration, safeguarding of rare plants etc), canal towpaths and most beaches. By custom, though not by right, you are generally free to walk across the open and uncultivated higher land of mountain, moorland and fell, but this varies from area to area and from one season to another – grouse moors, for example, will be out of bounds during the breeding and shooting seasons and some open areas are used as Ministry of Defence firing ranges, for which reason access will be restricted. In some areas the situation has been clarified as a result of 'access agreements' made between the landowners and either the county council or the national park authority, which clearly define when and where you can walk over such open country.

 ### Safety on the Hills

The hills, mountains and moorlands of Britain, though of modest height compared with those in many other countries, need to be treated with respect. Friendly and inviting in good weather, they can quickly be transformed into wet, misty, windswept and potentially dangerous areas of wilderness in bad weather. Even on an outwardly fine and settled summer day, conditions can rapidly deteriorate. In winter, of course, the weather can be even more erratic and the hours of daylight are much shorter.

Therefore it is advisable to always take both warm and waterproof clothing, sufficient nourishing food, a hot drink, first-aid kit, torch and whistle. Wear suitable footwear, ie. strong walking boots or shoes that give a good grip over rocky terrain and on slippery slopes. Try to obtain a local weather forecast and bear it in mind before you start. Do not be afraid to abandon your proposed route and return to your starting point in the event of a sudden and unexpected deterioration in the weather. Do not go alone. Allow enough time to finish the walk well before nightfall.

Most of the walks described in this book do not venture into remote wilderness areas and will be safe to do, given due care and respect, at any time of year in all but the most unreasonable weather. Indeed, a crisp, fine winter day often provides perfect conditions for walking, with firm ground underfoot and a clarity that it is not possible to achieve in the other seasons of the year. A few walks in this book, however, are suitable only for reasonably fit and experienced hill walkers who are able to use a compass, and these routes should definitely not be tackled by anyone else during the winter months or in bad weather, especially high winds and mist. These are indicated in the general description that precedes each of the walks.

 ### Useful Organisations

Council for National Parks
246 Lavender Hill, London SW11 1LJ.
Tel. 020 7924 4077

Snowdonia National Park Authority
National Park Authority, Penrhyndeudraeth, Gwynedd LL48 6LS.
Tel. 01766 770274
National Park information centres:
Aberdyfi: 01654 767321
Betws-y-Coed: 01690 710426
Blaenau Ffestiniog: 01766 830360
Dolgellau: 01341 422888
Harlech: 01766 780658
Llanberis: 01286 870765

Snowdonia Society
Capel Curig, Gwynedd. Tel. 01690 720787

Council for the Protection of Rural Wales
Tŷ Gwyn, 31 High Street,
Welshpool, Powys SY21 7YD.
Tel. 01938 552525/556212

Countryside Agency
John Dower House, Crescent Place,
Cheltenham, Gloucestershire GL50 3RA.
Tel. 01242 521381

Countryside Council for Wales
Plas Penrhos, Ffordd Penrhos,
Bangor, Gwynedd LL5 72LQ.
Tel. 01248 370444

Forestry Commission
Information Dept, 231 Corstorphine Road,
Edinburgh EH12 7AT.
Tel. 0131 334 0303

Long Distance Walkers' Association
Bank House, High Street, Wrotham,
Sevenoaks, Kent TN15 7AE
Tel. 01732 883705

National Trust
Membership and general enquiries:
PO Box 39, Bromley, Kent BR1 3XL.
Tel. 020 8315 1111
National Trust Office for Wales
Trinity Square, Llandudno,
Gwynedd LL30 2DE. Tel. 01492 860123

Ordnance Survey
Romsey Road, Maybush,
Southampton SO16 4GU.
Tel. 08456 05 05 05 (Lo-call)

Ramblers' Association (main office)
2nd Floor, Camelford House, 87–90 Albert
Embankment, London SE1 7TW.
Tel. 020 7339 8500

Ramblers' Association (Wales)
Tŷ'r Cerddwyr, High Street,
Gresford, Wrexham LL12 8PT.
Tel. 01978 855148
Wales Tourist Board
Brunel House, 2 Fitzalan Road,
Cardiff CF2 1UY. Tel. 029 2049 9909
*Tourist information centres (*not open all year):*
*Bala: 01678 521021
Bangor: 01248 352786

Betws-y-Coed: 01690 710426
*Blaenau Ffestiniog: 01766 830360
*Conwy: 01492 592248
*Corris: 01654 761244
Dolgellau: 01341 422888
*Llanberis: 01286 870765
Llandudno: 01492 876413
Llangollen: 01978 860828
*Mold: 01352 759331
Porthmadog: 01766 512981
Rhyl: 01745 355068
Ruthin: 01824 703992
Wrexham: 01978 292015

Youth Hostels Association
Trevelyan House, Dimple Road, Matlock,
Derbyshire DE4 3YH
Tel. 01692 592600 (general enquiries)

 ### Ordnance Survey Maps of Snowdonia
North Wales, Snowdon and Offa's Dyke are
covered by Ordnance Survey 1:50 000
(1¼ inches to 1 mile or 2cm to 1km) scale
Landranger map sheets 115, 116, 117, 124, 125
and 126. These all-purpose maps are packed
with information to help you explore the area
and show viewpoints, picnic sites, places of
interest and caravan and camping sites.

To examine the area in more detail, and
especially if you are planning walks,
Ordnance Survey Explorer maps at 1:25 000
(2½ inches to 1 mile or 4cm to 1km) scale
are ideal:

OL17 (Snowdon)
OL18 (Harlech, Porthmadog & Bala)
OL23 (Cadir Idris & Llyn Tegid)
240 (Oswestry)
255 (Llangollen & Berwyn)
256 (Wrexham)
263 (Anglesey East)
264 (Vale of Clwyd)
265 (Clwydian Range)
266 (Wirral & Chester)

To get to North Wales use the Ordnance
Survey Great Britain Route Travel map at
1:625 000 (1 inch to 10 miles or 1cm to
6.25km) scale or Road Travel map 6 (Wales
and West Midlands) at 1:250 000 (1 inch to
4 miles or 1cm to 2.5km) scale.

Ordnance Survey maps and guides are
available from most booksellers, stationers
and newsagents.

www.totalwalking.co.uk

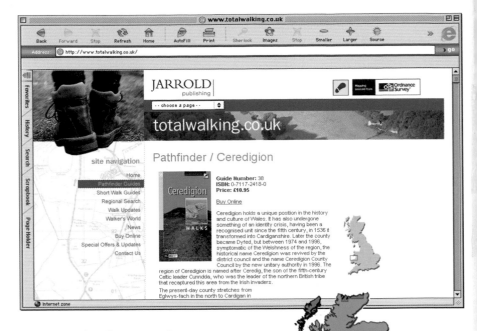

www.totalwalking.co.uk
is the official website of the Jarrold
Pathfinder and Short Walks guides. This
interactive website features a wealth of
information for walkers – from the latest
news on route diversions and advice from
professional walkers to product news, free
sample walks and promotional offers.